T0171432

First I AM

An Introduction to the

HIGHER SELF IMAGE, MIND, BODY & LIFE!

Melissa Dunn & Leah Dunn

ISBN: 978-1-4525-3926-3 (e)
ISBN: 978-1-4525-3900-3 (sc)
ISBN: 978-1-4525-3899-0 (hc)

Library of Congress Control Number: 2011915915

Balboa Press books may be ordered through booksellers or by contacting:

Balboa Press
A Division of Hay House
1663 Liberty Drive
Bloomington, IN 47403
www.balboapress.com
1-(877) 407-4847

Printed in the United States of America

Balboa Press rev. date: 9/20/2011

On September 19, 1982 Linda Perry wrote the following entry in her diary:

> Help me dear Lord to learn from my mistakes so I can help others. I don't know why I feel led to write these things down but maybe this will help someone else someday!

Mom,

This book and all the subsequent materials that will accompany this book are due, in part, to your "mistakes." Thank God for those mistakes, for without them—*all of them*—the wisdom contained within this material wouldn't have been possible. Because of your *life,* many will be made whole! Your *someday* is now! Congratulations Mom—you did it!

We love and miss you more than words . . .

Trust in the LORD with all thine heart; and lean not unto thine own understanding. In all thy ways acknowledge him, and he shall direct thy paths.

Proverbs 3:5-6

Contents

Scripture Reference Key

NIV	The New International Version
KJV	The King James Version
MSG	The Message Bible
NLT	The New Living Translation
BBEV	The Bible in Basic English Version
CEV	The Contemporary English Version
DARBY	The Darby Translation

Introduction

The Yet

When we lose sight of our *First I AM* self image—God's glorious image in our mind and body—we lose balance for our lives. Without proper balance, we find ourselves and our lives dis-eased and dis-ordered. Frankly, we find ourselves upside down.

While writing this book, we attempted to hold fast to our own *First I AM* self. We found that the world at large is a war zone; offering every opportunity to disbelieve God and his plan for our lives. It's easy to let go of God's image for the image and likeness of fleshly man. Pity parties are designed by man, and losing one's true *I AM* image is what gives a pity party its real fuel.

We lost our parents to disease and disorder, we were estranged from our immediate and extended family members, our retirement funds were depleted due to a diseased economy, our ability to borrow cash became impossible, and even some of our friends turned their backs on us. But more frightening than the aforementioned losses; we began to lose sight of our vision for this program and for our own *First I AM* higher self image and likeness.

Losing hope affected our minds and our bodies—more specifically, our physical, mental, and spiritual balance. More often than not, we found ourselves dominated entirely by our lower emotional minds—which made perfect sense, considering that we were in a constant state of survival rather than belief and faith in our *higher self image* in God. We had long forgotten things like Philippians 4:13 and Jeremiah 29:11. We were reacting defensively day in and day out. We were trying to stay alive.

Just as soon as one wave of adversity would come crashing in around us, another and still another would come rolling in at us. We would barely reach the surface for a quick gulp of air before being forcibly pulled under by another undertow of misfortune. There were times when we even lost our grip on one another—the pain and stress proved to be greater than we could bear. And then, there was the word *yet.*

Romans 4:18-24

> Against all hope, Abraham in hope believed and so became the father of many nations, just as it had been said to him, "So shall your offspring be." Without weakening in his faith, he faced the fact that his body was as good as dead—since he was about a hundred years old—and that Sarah's womb was also dead. *Yet* he did not waver through unbelief regarding the promise of God, but was strengthened in his faith and gave glory to God, being fully persuaded that God had power to do what he had promised. This is why "it was credited to him as righteousness." The words "it was credited to him" were written not for him alone, but also for us, to whom God will credit righteousness—for us who believe in him. (NIV)

The word *yet* of Romans 4:20 is what caught our attention. Yes, we were tossed to and fro upon the waves of this tumultuous life, *yet* we decided to hold onto God's promises. God had promised us something long before our earthly material losses—something much higher than our lower minds could even comprehend! God had planted within us *His* very image and likeness! With God's image and likeness came His power, dominion, authority, and strength over our seemingly impossible circumstances! God gave us His dream, His hope, and His future design for our lives just as his word had asserted in Jeremiah 29:11. God had imbued us with His strength and resilience just like his word had declared in Philippians 4:13. We found ourselves to be more than conquerors just as Romans 8:37 affirmed.

And then there was Job. Job, when faced with his adversity said, "though He slay me, *yet* will I wait for and trust Him and I have no hope—nevertheless, I will maintain and argue my ways before Him and even to His face."[1] We had determined, like Job, that though God was allowing life to beat against our backs and strip us of our material possessions and family, we would argue our case before him night and day until relief was attained. Like Job, we knew *who* and *what* we were—we had simply forgotten momentarily, due to the intense pain and suffering we were experiencing. Nevertheless, *Yet* was on our side.

The Journey Is the Destination

Over the last thirty-five years, we have read self-help books until we are blue in the face. The most frustrating part about these books is how long the author goes on identifying the problem; saying the same things over and over again, as though it were a nightmare infomercial that never ends. Why won't they just tell us how to order the product or, better yet, how to fix the problem?

For this exhausting reason, we want to tell you, before you get started reading our book, that this entire book is a definition—a long definition, but a definition all the same. Why such a long definition? We believe that in order to really understand where you're going you must first identify where you've been and where you currently are. When you are lost and you want to find "your desired destination" the first thing you do is find the "you are here" mark. Not only is this book *your* "you are here" mark, but it represents "your desired destination."

What we have learned is this: the journey is the destination. The destination is *higher self* awareness. The best way to experience *higher self* awareness is allowing your *self* to *be* in the moment—aware of the *higher self* at all times—not at some later pre-destined time.

---

1 Job 13:15

This explains why other authors have said the same things over and over and over, so we, the students of *self*, can immerse ourselves in the gift of just simply *being*. We humans have become so over-identified with our *human-ness* that we've lost sight of our *being-ness*.

So please indulge us while we define *your* current location. You might just discover that you have already arrived at "your desired destination." We are confident that the wisdom provided in these lessons will serve as an invaluable tool and resource to those who truly desire to be made whole and liberated—mind, body, and spirit!

Chapter 1

RETHINKING GENESIS

The word *Genesis* means *beginning or origin.* The Old and New Testaments of our Bible represent the story of our spiritual *beginning,* just as our physical genetics tell the story of our physical *origin.* Consequently, both our spiritual and physical genesis are intertwined as proven by scientific and spiritual minds. Quite literally, God is in the details of all matter—materially and spiritually.

If we "believers" expect to make a dramatic impact on our world for the sake of God's overall divine plan for mankind, then we must rethink the book of Genesis and our former beliefs and interpretations. More importantly, we must be willing to rethink our own physical genesis. Materially speaking, we are a totality of our genetic ancestry. Every gene, protein, and chemical in our body tells a unique story about who we were in not only our recent past, but more significantly, our distant and ancient past.

Sobering but Not Surprising

We wish we had a nickel for every friend that has said to us, "I left the faith of my youth because . . . " Most of our clients have given up on their religious beliefs because it proved to be too hard—too restrictive—too incongruent with their spirit. It appears that what we were hearing was being validated by several surveys concerning today's youth.

According to America's Research Group, Americans under thirty years of age are rejecting the Christian faith in unprecedented numbers.[2] In fact, what the numbers suggest is not a slow move away from the Christian faith, but rather a hurried mass exodus. Ninety-five percent of those polled attended church regularly during their elementary and middle school years, however, only 55 percent attended church regularly during their high school years, with only 11 percent attending church into their college years.[3]

The ARG survey discovered the following reasons for the mass departure from faith by today's youth:

- Nearly 40 percent said they first doubted the Bible's authenticity in middle school.
- 43.7 percent said they first doubted the Bible's authenticity during their high school years.
- Only around 10 percent said they first became doubtful about Bible accounts during college.
- 61 percent said they attended Sunday school, while 39 percent said they didn't.
- Those who attended Sunday school were more likely:

    - not to believe that all the accounts and stories in the Bible are true
    - to doubt the Bible because it was written by men
    - to defend keeping abortion legal
    - to accept the legalization of gay marriage
    - to believe in evolution
    - to believe that good people don't need to go to church

---

2 http://thetruthwins.com/archives/mass-exodus-staggering-numbers-of-americas-young-people-are-rejecting-the-christian-faith (accessed April 27, 2010)

3 http://www.christianpost.com/news/survey-churches-losing-youths-long-before-college-39433/ (accessed June 29, 2009)

Furthermore, among those who said they do not believe in the authenticity of the Bible, the following reasons were given:

- 24 percent said it was written by men
- 18 percent said it was not translated correctly
- 15 percent said the Bible contradicts itself
- 14 percent said modern science is incompatible with the Genesis narrative

The survey found that attending Sunday school proved to be of no help in strengthening a young person's faith. In fact, the survey revealed that Sunday school is actually more likely to be detrimental to the spiritual and moral health of children.

In yet another new survey of 1,200 eighteen—to twenty-nine-year-olds, Lifeway Christian Resources[4] found that 72 percent felt they were "really more spiritual than religious." The survey also discovered the following statistics:

- 65 percent rarely or never pray with others, and 38 percent almost never pray by themselves either.
- 65 percent rarely or never attend worship services.
- 67 percent don't read the Bible or sacred texts.

According to the American Religious Identification Survey conducted by the Institute for the Study of Secularism in Society & Culture at Trinity College, 46 percent of Americans say they have no religion.[5] However, having no religious affiliation doesn't necessarily mean young people between the ages of eighteen and thirty-give are non-believers. According to a survey by Bohan Advertising/Marketing, the Barna Group, and the United Methodist Church, 62 percent of

4 http://www.usatoday.com/news/religion/2010-04-27-1Amillfaith27_ST_N.htm

5 Trinity College Hartford Connecticut

eighteen to thirty-four-year-olds consider themselves to be spiritual rather than religious.[6]

For the most part, these statistics are not surprising, however, as we mentioned earlier, 67 percent of those polled (eighteen to twenty-nine years of age) by the Lifeway Christian Resource survey admitted that they seldom read their Bible or other religious texts. Of all the statistics that we discovered regarding the religious climate of young people in America today, this statistic disturbed us the most.

We believe that people (young or otherwise) are rejecting the wisdom and truths of the Bible because of literal and fundamentalist interpretations of Scripture by former generations. What these stats are really saying is this: young people are being led by their spiritual vibration rather than by their religious ancestor's fundamentalist and literalist beliefs and traditions. This isn't a bad thing.

We have found that our clients and students who have left the faith of their youth do so because they have matured psychologically and spiritually. In short, they have changed their minds about what they believe, and rightfully so. Although many find fundamentalism's death a bit disconcerting, we believe it falls in line with the natural evolution and progression of man's mind renewal and soul regeneration journey.[7] We also feel that fundamentalism's death is completely compatible with biblical truth.[8]

Got Questions?

After reading the first two chapters of Genesis, any serious student of the Bible will come away with more questions than answers. For instance, in Genesis chapter 1 God creates everything before he creates man. However, in the Genesis chapter 2 creation narrative, God creates

6 UMCOM—*The Re-think Church Workshop*

7 1 Corinthians 13:11-23

8 Revelation 18:4

man first. In the Genesis 1 narrative mankind is created after the image and likeness of God, whereas in Genesis 2, mankind is formed from the dust of the earth. So what gives? Are there two creation narratives, or one? Modern scholarship believes it has come up with the answer.

Traditionally speaking, most every fundamentalist has been taught that the Bible is the inspired and infallible Word of God. As a matter of fact, most fundamentalists believe that all of the stories in the Bible happened just as they were written—literally. The serpent really did speak to Eve, the whale really did swallow Jonah, Lot's wife really did turn into a pillar of salt, and Elijah really did call fire down from heaven. However, liberal students of the Bible view the stories as myth, allegory, and legends intended to lead one toward spiritual enlightenment and self-awareness.

Literalists and fundamentalists believe that Moses wrote the first five books of the Old Testament referred to as the *Pentateuch.* However, modern liberal scholarship accepts the Pentateuch as a *composite work.* Scholars believe that the Pentateuch is the work of many authors, not just one. More specifically, modern scholars believe that Genesis chapter 1 and Genesis chapter 2 were composed by more than one author. This belief is known as the *JEDP Theory.*

In short, the JEDP theory states that the first five books of the Bible—Genesis, Exodus, Leviticus, Numbers, and Deuteronomy—were written by different authors. This theory is largely based upon the fact that the Genesis 1 and Genesis 2 narratives employ different names for God, which are used in various places throughout the Pentateuch. In addition, there are acute differences in the linguistic style of the varying texts.

The letters J-E-D-P stand for the four alleged authors. For instance, there is one supposed author who employs the name *Jehovah* for God's name, and another uses the name *Elohim.* Thus, the letters J and E are used respectively. There is the assumed author of the **D**euteronomy text, and another believed to be a **p**riestly author of the book of Leviticus. Thus, the use of the letters D and P. In addition, the scholars who created the JEDP theory believe that the Pentateuch was likely written and/or compiled around the fourth century BC.

While scholarship is helpful and needful for a host of varying reasons, we believe that scholarship tends to lean toward an academic approach entirely, whereas we believe that biblical interpretation can only be acquired via the use of the spiritual mind.[9] When an individual attempts to understand that which is spiritual from a purely intellectual and natural mindset, the spiritual interpretation is lost. This, we believe, is the reason for biblical illiteracy among the young and the old of our nation. We also believe that the Bible holds the key to all of life's questions; however, most will never find the life-transforming answers to their toughest questions, because they fear they will never understand their Bible. Sadly, they are right.

The natural mind cannot comprehend the deep things of Spirit.[10] In addition, genuine biblical revelation knowledge, which, by the way, is spiritual wisdom imparted, will never be achieved through a fundamentalist and literalist rendering. The *First IAM* teaching series requires the employment of one's spiritual mind. Thus, before one can understand the *First IAM* principles, a consideration to suspend one's old literalist and fundamentalist beliefs must be contemplated long and hard. It has been our experience that letting go of these old religious beliefs and traditions will prove easier said than done. Nonetheless, it can be done, for these two authors have proven it.

A Young or Old Earth?

As children growing up in a fundamentalist protestant belief system, we were taught the "young Earth" creationism theory (YEC). YEC

9 1 Corinthians 2:10

10 1 Corinthians 2

is a form of creation that asserts the universe and all living organisms were created by God during a very short period of time (between 5,700 and 10,000 years ago). We were taught that God created the universe and all living organisms in six twenty-four-hour periods. In essence, we were taught a very literalist interpretation of Genesis 1 and 2.

However, as we entered the public school system, we learned a very different view of creationism. We learned that Earth was much older than a few thousand years, and that most of the life forms on earth weren't created in six twenty-four-hour periods, but rather they had evolved over billions of years through a process known as natural selection. We noticed something very disconcerting about our fundamentalist beliefs; all of the information we were receiving through our science and biology classes at school had been verified by the fields of geology, paleontology, and astronomy, whereas a young Earth creationism theory had no evidence to substantiate its claims except for a few verses in the first two chapters of the Bible. We surmised that a fundamentalist and literalist interpretation of the Genesis narrative might explain why 67 percent of those polled by the Lifeway Christian Resources Survey don't read their Bibles and no longer affiliate with the religion of their youth.

Two Stories or One?

So, what do we believe about the Genesis creation narrative differences; differences which modern scholarship believes can be answered best by attributing them to manifold authorship while science believes it's all a matter of evolution and natural selection? In short, while we believe that there is a strong indication that more than one author contributed to the Pentateuch and that the earth is much older than we were led to believe, we do not believe that there is more than one creation narrative. On the contrary, we believe that there is one creation narrative, but two very different lives being illustrated. We also believe that the life one chooses to abide in has the potential to create one's perceptions about one's self-value,

God-value, world-value, and ultimately, one's life-value. In short, we believe how an individual interprets the Genesis creation narrative can mean the difference between departing from the faith of their youth, or deciding to stay the course.

Energy of Unity

Earlier, we discussed some pretty alarming statistics concerning the mass exodus of today's youth regarding their former religious beliefs and faith. We need to make clear that the eighteen—to thirty-year-olds that were polled aren't leaving the church because of the Bible; they're leaving the church because of the flawed biblical interpretation of men, and more specifically, the Genesis narrative. Many young adults feel that the church's young earth interpretation is incompatible with modern scientific evidence.

In addition, they are turned off by fundamentalism's elitism, self righteous beliefs, and intolerance. Many of these young people are closer to the Spirit's vibrational energy field than we old codgers, meaning that the beliefs and interpretation of fundamentalists and literalists are entirely incongruent with the energy of unity they feel within themselves versus the negative energy of disunity and divisiveness of the earth. This kind of attitude and belief-set is extremely off-putting to these spiritually *all-inclusive* young adults.

That's why the *First IAM*® and *IAM*Renewed4Life® programs are so important, not only to the younger generations, but also for the older generations who have moved closer to spirituality versus the institution of organized religion. Through a series of spirit-based programs, we strip away the old interpretations and beliefs that are based upon fear and shame and replace them with the beauty of Scripture through the leadership of the Spirit of grace and truth.

God Is Spirit

God is spirit and if the Bible is truly God's Word, then the words of the Bible are words of spirit. Paul asserts in 1 Corinthians 2 that the deep things of the Spirit (God's word and ideas) must be discerned by the spiritual mind. A literal interpretation of the Bible from a purely literal posture will not yield a spiritual truth or hidden mystery of God. The natural mind finds the deep things of God to be foolishness. This might explain why young adults are leaving the church in mass numbers, because of the "foolish" and "natural" reading and interpretations of Scripture.

We find that these young people are justified in their exodus, for even God commands us to come away from these types of idolatrous religious practices and beliefs.[11] Fundamentalism is built upon the faulty foundations of fear and shame; driven by the lower minds of man. Fear and shame are *not* disciplines of God. Fear and shame are the result of a low and poor self concept created by emotional minds. A poor self concept is the fruit of a false self-obsessed life rather than a life lived by a true spiritual self image.

First IAM Renewal

We can do something about the inner conflict between our faith and our logic. We can begin the renewal process by allowing the Spirit of God to interpret Scripture through us. We can take full responsibility for our spiritual growth and development. So often—too often—we Christians allow fallible men to educate us in the ways of God. This has to stop! You cannot receive spiritual revelation by proxy. Wisdom and discernment are gifts and must be experienced and understood personally.

Something else we can do is to begin thinking about thinking. Many of us think without self awareness. It's important to become aware

[11] Revelation 18:4

of who is doing the thinking in our heads. In addition, we need to rethink our interpretation and understanding of the old Genesis creation narrative. We believe that the creation narrative of Genesis holds the vital keys to our true identity *(First IAM)* which can provide for us a long and prosperous life. Thus, it is mandatory that we reexamine the Genesis narrative texts prudently. With that being said, let's do just that: reexamine our Bible and our beliefs with a new mind, ear, and eye!

Chapter 2

THE *FIRST IAM* HIGHER SELF IMAGE

We demonstrated in the last chapter how a fundamentalist-literalist interpretation of the Genesis creation narrative, without the employment of reason, logic, and rationale, is facilitating a mass exodus of today's youth from the traditional Judeo-Christian beliefs of former generations. We have learned that flawed ideas and beliefs about one's universe, self, and God do indeed matter. Now that we have a better understanding of America's temperature regarding it's religiosity, let's turn our attention to the *First IAM higher self image*, an image that will not only change America, but the entire universe!

Who Do Men Say That *I AM*?[12]

First of all, before we define our true self image, it might be more prudent to determine how God defines our true self image. Genesis 1:26-27 holds the answer to our question.

It reads,

> God said, Let us make man in our image, after our likeness: and let them have dominion over the fish of the sea, and over the fowl of the air, and over the cattle, and over all the earth, and over every creeping thing that creepeth upon the earth. So God created man

12 Mark 8:27

> in his own image, in the image of God created he him; male and female created he them. (KJV)

Thus, God defines mankind by his own image and likeness—his own standard and valuation system. So, what exactly is God's image and likeness?

John 4:24 holds the answer to this question. It reads,

> Your worship must engage your spirit in the pursuit of truth. That's the kind of people the Father is out looking for: those who are simply and honestly themselves before him in their worship. God is sheer being itself—Spirit. Those who worship him must do it out of their very being, their spirits, their true selves, in adoration. (MSG)

Based upon the aforementioned Scriptures, God defines mankind by his own *Spirit* and those who wish to be in relationship with God must do so from their *true* self image, which is Spirit.

Isaiah 55:8-9 reads,

> I don't think the way you think. The way you work isn't the way I work . . . For as the sky soars high above earth, so the way I work surpasses the way you work, and the way I think is beyond the way you think. (MSG)

God's ideas regarding any subject, not excluding his ideas regarding mankind, are much higher than the ideas of the earth. Therefore, any identity that God has set aside for mankind is a *higher identity*; a *higher self image*.

Romans 3:23 reads,

> For all have sinned; all fall short of God's glorious standard. (NLT)

Second Corinthians 3:16-18 reads,

> Whenever someone turns to the Lord, the veil is taken away. For the Lord is the Spirit, and wherever the Spirit of the Lord is, there is freedom. So all of us who have had that veil removed can see and reflect the glory of the Lord. And the Lord—who is the Spirit—makes us more and more like him as we are changed into his glorious image. (NLT)

God's glory is God's self image. God's self image is Spirit. According to Romans 3:23, we have all *fallen short* of God's glorious image in that, we have failed to retain God's image and likeness in our minds.[13] The Scripture also says that we have "sinned." The word *sin* in the Greek [*harmartano*] means to *err, to be mistaken, to miss the mark*.[14]

Thus, Romans 3:23 could read something like this,

> People have missed the point regarding God's wonderful image, and for this reason alone, they have fallen short of a successful and healthy life. [our emphasis]

Mankind defines himself by the lower things of the earth which are subordinate to God's image, likeness, and standard for successful living. Mankind defines himself by his own flesh and his earthly false images and labels (father, wage earner, executive, white, middle-class, male, etc.) rather than by his spiritual likeness (spirit—limitless, timeless, changeless, infinite, and immeasurable).

Genesis 1:27a and 1:27b

Genesis 1:27 reads,

> God created man in his own image, in the image of God created *he him*; male and female created *he them*. (KJV)

13 Romans 1:28

14 "Sin" Enhanced Strong's Lexicon #264

In order for the *higher self image* of God to be made distinct from the lower self image of man in this verse, we need to break up Genesis 1:27 into two separate segments, as follows:

a) God created man in his own image, in the image of God created *he him;*
b) male and female created *he them.*

The phrase *he him* of the first segment (designated as Genesis 1:27a) is the *higher self image* of God in mankind whereas the phrase *he them* of segment two (we designated as Genesis 1:27b) is the *lower material self image* of mankind.

The *higher self image* is man's spiritual identity which is singular (he him) in nature whereas the lower self image is man's physical identity which is plural (he them) in nature. God's nature is one of unity whereas man's lower nature is one of duality and disunity.

Psalm 8:3-9 says,

> When I consider thy heavens, the work of thy fingers, the moon and the stars, which thou hast ordained; what is man, that thou art mindful of *him*? And the son of man, that thou visitest *him*? For thou hast made *him* a little lower than the angels, and hast crowned *him*_with glory and honour. Thou madest *him* to have dominion over the works of thy hands; thou hast put all things under *his* feet: All sheep and oxen, yea, and the beasts of the field; The fowl of the air, and the fish of the sea, and whatsoever passeth through the paths of the seas. O LORD our Lord, how excellent is *thy name* in all the earth! (KJV)

In John 5:37-40 Jesus says,

> The Father who sent me has Himself testified concerning me. Not one of you has ever given ear to His voice or seen His form. You have always been deaf to His voice and blind to the vision of Him.

> And you have not His word (His thoughts) living in your hearts, because you do not believe and adhere to and trust in and rely on *Him* Whom He has sent. You search and investigate and pore over the Scriptures diligently, because you suppose and trust that you have eternal life through them. And these [very Scriptures] testify about me! And still you are not willing [but refuse] to come to me, so that you might have life. (AMP)

Our true identity and life rests in the *Him* of the Scriptures. Paul said it best in Ephesians 2:1-6. Paul asserts that many of us were once dead to our true nature in Spirit. But as we become increasingly aware of our *highest self image*; an image demonstrated through the life, death, resurrection, and teachings of the Christ, we begin to live by the precepts and value system of God versus the ideologies and value system of this earth. Those who are abiding in their *true* and *highest self image* are abiding "in the Christ image" which is the true image and likeness of God.[15] By following after the Christ's example, we are made perfect in God's image.[16] It is the Christ mind and self image which empowers us to do the things that God has purposed for us to accomplish while in the body.[17] The *Christ identity* is the totality of our divine being-ness—our true salvation.

Colossians 1 asserts that as we move away from the allure and lusts of this earth, we move further into the reality and realm of Spirit. We are told that the Christ (*Him*) is the "invisible image of God."[18] We are also told that God created everything in heaven and earth—seen and unseen—for the pleasure of this *Him* identity.[19] It is through this *higher identity* and *higher self image* that we find peace with God and man—our *higher life* and purpose. It's this message that the literalists and fundamentalists are missing—or as St. Peter asserted, they stumble

---

15 John 1:1; Colossians 1

16 John 17:22-23; 1 John 4:17-18

17 Romans 1:16; Philippians 4:13

18 Colossians 1:15

19 Colossians 1:16-17; Revelation 4:11

over.[20] John 1:12 says, "But as many as received *him, to them* gave *he power to become the sons of God*, even *to_them* that believe on *his_name*." Here we find the words, *them* and *him* together again. As we move closer and closer toward our God image and likeness, we become more and more like the *Him (Christ)* and less like the *them (false identities of man)* of the current earth economy. We also begin to receive the things of God—things that were planned and predestined for us since before the creation of the universe.[21] In addition, we soon become aware of our true name, a name that is, in reality, God's name—an identity of *One*.[22]

Called by God's Name[23]

One's name is one's identity. People associate a face with a name. A person's face is often times the only image we see. However, there is an image which we are failing to see, and a name we are failing to take for our own.

We are *the Sons of God*—the very image and likeness of God (Genesis 1:27a). Sadly, we have become entirely over-identified with the Genesis 1:27b likeness. But we are more than our secondary likeness. As we peel back the layers of Genesis chapters 1 through 4, we will discover a completely different interpretation of not only the creation narrative but all of Scripture. Remember, Scripture's purpose is to create in you complete health and wholeness; albeit, Scripture historically has been used to create within you a sense of fear and shame.[24]

The *First IAM*® and *IAM*Renewed4Life® programs through the leading of the Spirit of God were designed to remove all obstacles of fear and shame. The *First IAM*® and *IAM*Renewed4Life® programs were designed to bring you to a true self awareness of your *higher self*

---

20 John 5:39; 1 Peter 2:7-8

21 Ephesians 1

22 Deut 6:4

23 Isaiah 43:7

24 2 Timothy 3:15

and a working knowledge of the extravagant love of God. By becoming aware of this *higher self* we are able to fulfill God's purpose and design for our lives and thus, change the landscape of the earth.[25] God's kingdom and economy will at last fill the earth as we begin to change our minds about *who* and *what we really are.*[26]

As we have demonstrated, the Genesis 1:27a *higher self image* is the preeminent self; *crowned with glory and honor.* The *higher self image* is identified with God's name which we are told is the *I AM.*[27]

The Burning Bush of *Higher Self* Revelation

Anyone who attended Sunday school regularly as a child remembers the story of Moses and the burning bush told in Exodus chapter 3. The passage reads,

> NOW MOSES kept the flock of Jethro his father-in-law, the priest of Midian; and he led the flock to the back or west side of the wilderness and came to Horeb or Sinai, the mountain of God. The Angel of the Lord appeared to him in a flame of fire out of the midst of a bush; and he looked, and behold, the bush burned with fire, yet was not consumed. And Moses said, "I will now turn aside and see this great sight, why the bush is not burned." And when the Lord saw that he turned aside to see, God called to him out of the midst of the bush and said, "Moses, Moses!" And he said, "Here am I."
>
> God said, "Do not come near; put your shoes off your feet, for the place on which you stand is holy ground." Also He said, "I am the God of your father, the God of Abraham, the God of Isaac, and the God of Jacob." And Moses hid his face, for he was afraid to look at God.

---

25 Matthew 5:14-16; Ephesians 1:4; Galatians 5:16

26 Matthew 6:10

27 Matthew 1:23

> And the Lord said, "I have surely seen the affliction of My people who are in Egypt, and have heard their cry because of their taskmasters and oppressors; for I know their sorrows and sufferings and trials. And I have come down to deliver them out of the hand and power of the Egyptians and to bring them up out of that land to a land good and large, a land flowing with milk and honey [a land of plenty]—to the place of the Canaanite, the Hittite, the Amorite, the Perizzite, the Hivite, and the Jebusite. Now behold, the cry of the Israelites has come to Me, and I have also seen how the Egyptians oppress them. Come now therefore, and I will send you to Pharaoh, that you may bring forth My people, the Israelites, out of Egypt.
>
> And Moses said to God, "Who am I that I should go to Pharaoh and bring the Israelites out of Egypt?" God said, "I will surely be with you; and this shall be the sign to you that I have sent you: when you have brought the people out of Egypt, you shall serve God on this mountain [Horeb, or Sinai]." And Moses said to God, "Behold, when I come to the Israelites and say to them, the God of your fathers has sent me to you, and they say to me, what is His name? What shall I say to them?" And God said to Moses, "I AM WHO I AM and WHAT I AM, and I WILL BE WHAT I WILL BE;"_and He said, "You shall say this to the Israelites: I AM has sent me to you!"
>
> God said also to Moses, "This shall you say to the Israelites: The Lord, the God of your fathers, of Abraham, of Isaac, and of Jacob, has sent me to you! This is My name forever, and by this name I am to be remembered to all generations. (AMP)

What a wonderful and beautiful illustration of what it looks like when we first come face to face with our *higher self image*. The *I AM* is God's name—God's identity. But what does that have to do with us?

Genesis 4:26 says,

> And Seth had a son, and he gave him the name of Enosh: at this time men first made use of the name of the Lord in worship. (BBEV)

Isaiah 43:6-7 says,

> I will say to the north, Give up; and to the south, Keep not back: bring my sons from far, and my daughters from the ends of the earth; every one that is called by my name: for I have created him for my glory, I have formed him; yea, I have made him. (AMP)

For one to say that "I AM God" is to commit the heinous offense of blasphemy according to religious men. When Jesus said, "Before Abraham was, I AM" in the gospel of John[28], the religious rulers of his day took up stones to kill him. Do we, mere human beings, dare call ourselves by God's name or worse yet; claim to be one with Spirit? Jesus did and so did the apostles Paul and John as made evident by the following Scriptures:

John 14:20

> I am in my Father are one, and you are in me, and I am in you. (AMP)

John 17:22-23

> And the glory which you gave me I have given to them; that they may be one, even as we are one: I in them, and you in me, that they may be made one with you. (KJV)

Romans 12:5

> So we, being many, are one body in Christ, and every one members one of another. (KJV)

---

[28] John 8:58

First Corinthians 10:17

For we being many are one bread, and one body: for we are all partakers of that one bread. (KJV)

First Corinthians 12:13

For by one Spirit are we all baptized into one body, whether we be Jews or Gentiles, whether we be bond or free; and have been all made to drink into one Spirit. (KJV)

First Corinthians 3:16

Know you not that you are the temple of God, and that the Spirit of God dwelleth in you? (KJV)

Ephesians 4:4-6

There is one body, and one Spirit, even as you are called in one hope of your calling; One Lord, one faith, one baptism, One God and Father of all, who is above all, and through all, and is in you all. (KJV)

First Corinthians 6:20

For you are bought with a price: therefore glorify God in your body, and in your spirit, which are God's. (KJV)

Acts 17:28

For in him [God] we live, and move, and have our being; as certain also of your own poets have said, For we are also his offspring. (KJV)

Many great mystics and theologians of earlier generations believed and taught that all men are called by God's name and live within God's identity. As a matter of fact, one of the greatest theologians of our history, John Wesley (1703-1791) had this commentary to make about Genesis 4:26:

> *The worshippers of God began to distinguish themselves*: so the margin reads it. Then began men to be *called by the name of the Lord, or,*

> *to call themselves by it.* Now Cain and those that had deserted religion had built a city, and begun to declare for irreligion, and called themselves the sons of men. Those that adhered to God began to declare for him and his worship, and *called themselves the sons of God.*[29]

Sadly, many of these brave men and women who declared their *I AM* God identity and unity were persecuted, imprisoned, brought before magistrates and popes, even tortured and crucified for making such heretical declarations. "All things are interdependent," wrote the fourteenth-century German theologian Meister Eckhart, for whom God is the unifying "Being of all beings."[30] However, not everyone agreed with Meister Eckhart.

We suspect that what these early mystics and spiritual teachers proclaimed for themselves is exactly what Moses understood for himself—*eventually.* As carefully demonstrated in the first few chapters of Exodus, it took Moses some time before he became comfortable with his new *I AM* identity. It's important to understand that when individuals, mystics or otherwise, make the declaration, "I *am* God," they're not claiming to be God but rather, they are attesting to and calling forth the truest and highest nature of their inner self, and it's this image and likeness that they identify with the most—the *I AM* part of their *higher self* constitution. They are distinguishing for themselves the infinite and boundless essence of the true self which can only be found in the "I *am*" of God just as John Wesley asserted in his commentary on Genesis 4:26. In addition, by asserting our *I AM* image and likeness (identity), we are entering into a state of graciousness, humility, and thankfulness to God. To think that God has filled us with his very nature—his glorious image and likeness—is enough to humble anyone. Therefore, we demonstrate our thankfulness by living our God-nature openly before all men with confidence.

---

29 http://www.kingjamesbibleonline.org/1611_Genesis-4-26/ (accessed May 2010)

30 http://www.theself.com/christianity.cfm (accessed May 2010)

The contemporary scholar and mystic Thomas Merton (1915-1968) put it this way,

> To say that I am made in the image of God is to say that love is the reason for my existence, for God is love. Love is my true identity. Selflessness is my true self. Love is my true character. Love is my name. [31]

To continue with our exegesis of Exodus 3:14, what God is really saying to Moses is this: "Moses, *I AM in you and you can't escape me. Wherever you go and whatever you do, I AM. Don't be afraid, I AM with you always.*"

Psalm 139:1-8 says it like this,

> O LORD, you have searched me [thoroughly] and have known me. You know my downsitting and my uprising; you understand my thought afar off. You sift and search out my path and my lying down, and you are acquainted with all my ways. For there is not a word in my tongue [still unuttered], but, behold, O Lord, You know it altogether. You have beset me and shut me in—behind and before, and you have laid your hand upon me. Your [infinite] knowledge is too wonderful for me; it is high above me, I cannot reach it. Where could I go from Your Spirit? Or where could I flee from your presence? If I ascend up into heaven, you are there; if I make my bed in Sheol (the place of the dead), behold, you are there. (AMP)

God is the *I AM* and wherever we go, we carry the *I AM* within us. *God dwells within you, as you.*[32] We are the image and likeness of God.[33]

---

31 "Thomas Merton Quotes," *Wikipedia, the Free Encyclopedia,* http://en.wikiquote.org/w/index.php?title = ThomasMerton&oldid= 13112376 (accessed May 5, 2011)

32 Elizabeth Gilbert *Eat, Pray, Love,* (New York: Penguin Group, 2006), page 191

33 Genesis 1:27

However, like Moses, we often choose to believe that God is a separate entity from ourselves—a God somewhere out there, or up there—before we accept our *I AM* image and identity. Perhaps this explains why Moses failed to enter the promised land: he failed to reflect and believe in his own God *I AM* image.

Numbers 20:7-12 reads,

> The Lord said to Moses, "You and Aaron must take the staff and assemble the entire community. *As the people watch, speak to the rock* over there, and it will pour out its water. You will provide enough water from the rock to satisfy the whole community and their livestock."
>
> So Moses did as he was told. He took the staff from the place where it was kept before the Lord. Then he and Aaron summoned the people to come and gather at the rock. "Listen, you rebels!" he shouted. "Must we bring you water from this rock?" Then *Moses raised his hand and struck the rock twice* with the staff, and water gushed out. So the entire community and their livestock drank their fill.
>
> But the Lord said to Moses and Aaron, "Because *you did not trust me enough to demonstrate my holiness to the people* of Israel, you will not lead them into the land *I am* giving them!" (NLT)

Moses wasn't commanded to strike the rock. Moses was told to speak to the rock. Not only did Moses strike the rock—he struck twice. We each have one fundamental and common purpose in life: to be a reflection of God's glory in the earth. God's glory is his spiritual image and likeness—our true nature—our *I AM* identity! When we, like Moses, fail to believe the *I AM,* we fail to live the *First IAM higher life*—a *life* promised and designed of God.

Proverbs 18:21 says,

> Words kill, words give life; they're either poison or fruit—you choose. (MSG)

Our mouths wield a tremendous amount of power.

Luke 6:45 says,

> What you say flows from what is in your heart. (NLT)

What we really think comes pouring out of our mouths. It appears that Moses' mouth gushed with unbelief, which proved to be greater than the water which poured from the rock. You can't fool God, nor can you fool others. *Who* and *what* we believe ourselves to be gushes from our mouths. But don't lose heart—literally—there's still time to change not only our mind, but our mouth also!

First Corinthians 3:16 reads,

> Know ye not that ye are the temple of God, and that the Spirit of God dwelleth in you? (KJV)

Romans 12:1-2 reads,

> I plead with you to give your bodies to God. Let them be a living and holy sacrifice—the kind he can use. When you think of what he has done for you, is this too much to ask? Don't copy the behavior and customs of this world, but let God transform you into a new person by changing the way you think. Then you will know what God wants you to do and you will know how good and pleasing and perfect his will really is. (NLT)

Our clay material body is the vessel God chooses to house his image and likeness. If you knew how much power you truly possess, you'd treat your body with care and concern. You'd want to live as long as you could because as Paul asserts, *you would know just how pleasurable God's divine design for your life really is.* God created everything for his pleasure and we can enjoy that same pleasure—the very pleasure of God—if we will allow ourselves to accept our *I AM* identity.[34]

Those who refuse to receive their God image and likeness effectively and responsibly are like Moses striking the rock before the eyes of the Hebrews. It's a poor testimony of and witness to our own self esteem and our esteem of God. Your current life is a direct reflection of your core self concept and value. Your self esteem is a direct reflection of how you care for God's image and likeness. There are many who claim to love God but loathe themselves—their bodies—their lives. This is incongruent with biblical teaching. You cannot expect to enter into a life of abundance (the Kingdom of Heaven/Promised Land) while deliberately living by a false and low self image and concept. Thinking your *self* to be sub-standard or second is uncceptable.

Paul's Second Man—Our *First*

This *higher self image* is spoken of numerous times throughout the Hebrew Scriptures, and fully demonstrated and illustrated throughout the four canonical gospels as well as the various epistles of Paul and the teachings of the apostles of the early church era.

Paul asserts in 1 Corinthians 15:45-55

> It is written, the first man became a living being (an individual personality); the last man became a life-giving Spirit [restoring the dead to life]. But it is not the spiritual life which came first, but the physical and then the spiritual. The first man [was] from out of earth, made of dust (earthly-minded); the second Man [is from out of heaven. Now those who are made of the dust are like him who was first made of the dust (earthly-minded); and as is [the Man] from heaven, so also [are those] who are of heaven

34 Romans 8:28; Colossians 1:16; Revelation 4:11

> (heavenly-minded). And just as we have borne the image [of the man] of dust, so shall we and so let us also bear the image [of the Man] of heaven. But I tell you this, brethren, flesh and blood cannot [become whole mind, body and soul] inherit or share in the kingdom of God; nor does the perishable (that which is decaying) inherit or share in the imperishable (the immortal). Take notice! I tell you a mystery (a secret truth, an event decreed by the hidden purpose or counsel of God). We shall not all fall asleep [in death like the earthly minded-Adam], but we shall all be changed (transformed). In a moment, in the twinkling of an eye, at the [sound of the] last trumpet call [like the spiritually-minded Adam]. For a trumpet will sound, and the dead [in Christ] will be raised imperishable (free and immune from decay), and we shall be changed (transformed mind, body, and soul). For this perishable [part of us—our physical image and nature] must put on the imperishable [spiritual image and nature], and this mortal [part of us, this nature that is capable of dying] must put on immortality (freedom from death). And when this perishable puts on the imperishable and this that was capable of dying puts on freedom from death, then shall be fulfilled the Scripture that says, Death is swallowed up (utterly vanquished forever) in and unto victory. O death, where is your victory? O death, where is your sting? (AMP)

But wait a minute, didn't we just read in Genesis 1:27a that the "spiritual man" was created first? Yes we did. Then why is Paul asserting that the *higher self image* is the last man? Let's find out.

What Paul is saying, in our modern day English vernacular, is this: as humans, we become familiar with our lower natural and material self image first. But after we mature psychologically and spiritually (when we are transformed by the renewing of our mind in the Spirit of God), we become increasingly more familiar with our spiritual self image (*higher self image—I AM*). Our natural earthy self image, Paul's first Adam, is completely over-identified with his physical image and likeness (the earthly identity) whereas the spiritual self image, Paul's second Adam, is solely identified with his spiritual image and likeness (the God identity), which stays focused on the things of God rather than the things of man.

Paul goes onto say that there are some of us who live and act like the natural man (earthy) and there are those of us who are more spiritually (heavenly) attuned and aware. Not everyone becomes aware of their *higher self image* at the same time. Thus, we must demonstrate patience, compassion, and empathy toward those whose minds are not yet ready to be changed.

As time passes and as we become increasingly *higher self* aware, we will discover a *higher self image* waiting beneath our mortal bodies for transformation; our spiritual self image—our truest and highest self in God. With maturity, we cease identifying with our fleshly image in the mirror and begin seeking diligently for the God image and likeness within and without. Once we begin to identify with our *higher self image,* our decaying lower self image loses all meaning for us, and the threat of physical death loses its victory over our lives![35] This isn't just good news, this is great news!

The *I AM* versus the *AM I*

The body, mind, and spirit make up the whole *self.* The *First IAM* self is the *higher self image* fashioned after God's valuation system, whereas, the *lower self* image is that self which is created by the flawed, fear-based valuation system of mankind. Sadly, most of us, like Adam, operate from the *lower self image* for the better part of our lives—oblivious to the *higher self image* and its awesome potential.

As we mentioned earlier, the *higher self image* is the *First IAM.* The *First IAM* is a powerful, spiritually charged identity. The *First IAM* is our God image and likeness.[36] God is Spirit.[37] Spirit is light and light is a powerfully charged energy. When we become more aware

---

35 1 Corinthians 15:55

36 Genesis 1:27; 1 Corinthians 15:45-47

37 John 4:24; 1 John 1:5

(en-lightened) of this *higher self image*, our body and life become highly charged of Spirit's energy and wisdom.[38]

God is the *I am*, the ultimate and preeminent *First IAM* (Exodus 3:14). As we mentioned earlier, we believe the Genesis 1:27a man is mankind's spiritual self—his higher self image, his image defined by God—whereas the Genesis 1:27b man demonstrates man's physical self—his lower self image, the image which is defined by his world rather than by God's truth; an image we term the *AM I*.

We believe that most of us are living by our *AM I* self image versus our *I AM* self identity and likeness. The *AM I* self image by its very nature is one big question mark.[39] The *AM I* is the last half of the who, what, how, why, and when, whereas the *I AM* is the answer to all our questions and subsequent fears.

We believe that the *First IAM higher self image* enables an individual to attain a *First I AM* higher mind, higher body, and higher life. In like manner, we believe a lower and poor self image prevents one from attaining a higher existence because of the constant employment of the *AM I* lower mind, a lower body, and thus, a lower life.

The *AM I* Lower Self Image

The story of Adam and Eve is a wonderful narrative representing the spiritual evolutionary process of mankind.

Sadly, like Adam and Eve, we have believed our world and its varying opinions and laws concerning our personal identity and true self image. We have yielded and subjected our true nature to the sub-standard nature of labels, ideas, beliefs, prejudices, and value judgments of our culture and environment. Simply put, we have subordinated the glory

38 Job 32:8

39 Exodus 3:11

of God.[40] Paul speaks to this unhealthy subordination practice in his letter to the church at Rome.

Romans 1:16-25 reads,

> For I am not ashamed of the Good News about Christ. It is the power of God at work, saving [making everyone whole] who believes—the Jew first and also the Gentile.
>
> This Good News tells us how God makes us right in his sight. This is accomplished from start to finish by faith. As the Scriptures say, "It is through faith that a righteous person has life."
>
> . . . They know the truth about God because he has made it obvious to them. For ever since the world was created, people have seen the earth and sky. Through everything God made, they can clearly see his invisible qualities—his eternal power and divine nature. So they have no excuse for not knowing God.
>
> Yes, they knew God, but they wouldn't worship him as God or even give him thanks. And they began to think up foolish ideas of what God was like. As a result, their minds became dark and confused. Claiming to be wise, they instead became utter fools.
>
> . . . They traded the truth about God for a lie. So they worshiped and served the things God created instead of the Creator himself, who is worthy of eternal praise! Amen. (NLT)

Again, it's no surprise that Paul believes that the Christ life, death, resurrection, and identity represent the *power unto salvation* for all men. By becoming aware of and understanding our true identity (Genesis 1:27a) in Spirit, we are made whole—mind, body, and soul. He goes on further to say that those who refuse to become aware of their true self

---

40 Romans 1:23

image are holding God's image and likeness in *unrighteousness,* in a type of hostage situation. If you are not aware of your true nature and continue to behave from a purely literalist and fundamentalist mindset, you're grieving the Holy Spirit of God which resides within you. God's image and likeness is to be reflected in the earth, not withheld or buried![41] If we are not aware of the Spirit's existence, then we are holding the truth about God in an unhealthy way (unrighteousness).

How will others come to the knowledge of their own true self images and likenesses in God if we fail to see our own?[42] Paul says that we are without excuse—all of us! For the very invisible image and likeness of God is made clear by the works of God's hands in the things of nature, the human body, the universe, and more specifically, the human mind. Paul says that we have taken the incorruptible image of the Creator (God) and attempted to fashion it after the corruptible image of the creature (man). This type of behavior is idolatry. When we desire to look more like and act more like the subordinate things of this earth (i.e. flesh and blood) rather than seek after the higher things of God, we find ourselves following (worshiping) subordinate beliefs and traditions of depraved men lacking a God-image. Men with a corrupted God image find themselves living in poverty, disease, disorder, and darkness. One of the reasons why the institution of organized religion has remained a formidable foe of spirituality throughout the history of our nation is because religion thrives upon the poor, the illiterate, the depraved, and the spiritually ignorant. As soon as individuals make the conscious decision to become aware of their true self images and likenesses in Spirit, God clears away the cobwebs of false beliefs, psychological traumas, and strongholds of the once darkened minds.

Higher Self Individuation

We each begin life with one true nature: that which is Spirit, as is made evident by Genesis 1:27a. But as we grow and develop in our individual

41 Matthew 5:14-16

42 Psalm 67

environments, we begin to adopt other natures and images of our self (Genesis 1:27b), forgetting our *higher self image* and God likeness with the passage of time. These environmental, alternative, lower self images and/or identities influence our thinking, our attitudes, our beliefs, and our behaviors. However, historically speaking, as we mature and begin to employ reason and logic around the age of forty, we begin to examine these environmental lower images and/or identities more closely. As we perform these self introspections, we find that many things we once believed about ourselves and our world no longer apply or hold the same meaning or values. Psychology calls this type of personal examination process *individuation.* We laypeople call it the *mid-life crisis.* But is it really a crisis, or is it simply God knocking on the door of our hearts and minds, prodding us, saying, *you have dwelt long enough at this mountain. Turn and take your journey*?[43]

The process of individuation is *the act of making separate.*[44] In religious terms this type of process is referred to as *rebirth* or *sanctification.* If you recall from our introduction, 62 percent of the Barna survey group, considered themselves to be "spiritual" rather than "religious." We believe that these statistics are the result of the spiritual and psychological individuation process which appears to be on an accelerated trajectory. This is great news! In effect, this means that young people are coming into their *higher self images* at a much faster pace than ever before; long before mid-life occurs.

However, there are a few concerns we have for these young *First-IAMers.* We foresee the older fundamentalist demographic of society discomforting and discouraging these young people from true spiritual expansion and growth. In societal terms, most especially for the fundamentalists, the individuation process is considered unacceptable. This affirms the "misery loves company" adage. Much of society loves its group-think ideology because it's safe.

43 Deuteronomy 1:6

44 *Individuation* - Encarta Dictionary English North America (Version 2009)

Groupthink is a type of thought within a deeply cohesive in-group whose members try to minimize conflict and reach consensus without critically testing, analyzing, and evaluating ideas.[45] Sound familiar? Individual thought and differing beliefs and opinions threaten the clannish-type culture of Western society. Individuation at present seems to be a definite no-no for today's young spiritualists. Becoming one's *higher self image* may prove to be a secret pursuit as demonstrated by the lives of those who were a part of the early church era.

To continue, your past and current beliefs, ideas, and desires are the result of your individual universe and your ancestral and societal clan's group-think ideologies. Over time, you become a product of the clan—the tribe—essentially, the earth! You act like the clan, you talk like the clan, you dress like the clan, you smell like the clan, you walk like the clan, you believe like the clan, and worse still—you think like the clan! You are the clan—or so you come to believe![46] However, the person you believe yourself to be today is not the craftsmanship of God. On the contrary, the person you *perceive* yourself to be today is the handiwork of mankind and his fear-based value systems. Unfortunately, you have become so over-identified with your physical self and your ancestral origins that you have become an exact replica of those characteristics and attributes rather than reflecting your true spiritual traits and the divine design of God.[47]

Your beliefs, ideas, and desires don't have to be those of your ancestral and societal clan. You don't have to be the product of the clan—the tribe, the earth's flawed value system—anymore! You don't have to act like the clan, you don't have to talk like the clan, you don't have to dress like the clan, you don't have to smell like the clan, you don't have to walk like the clan, and better yet, *you don't have to think like the clan! You are not the clan—you are the very seed of God!*

---

45 "Group Think," *Wikipedia, the Free Encyclopedia,* http://en.wikipedia.org/wiki/Groupthink, (accessed April 3, 2011)

46 Proverbs 23:7

47 Psalm 139:14

First IAM Amnesia

The creation narrative of Genesis chapter 2 demonstrates the effects of losing sight of one's *higher self image.* The deep sleep of Adam is something that many of us have yet to understand. We would be willing to bet that most of you don't even know what we're referring to—this *Adam sleep.*

Genesis 2:18-25 reads,

> And the LORD *God said, "It is not good that the man should be alone*; I will make him a *helpmeet suitable for him.*"
>
> And out of the ground the LORD God formed every beast of the field and every fowl of the air; and brought them unto Adam to see what he would call them: and *whatsoever Adam called every living creature that was the name thereof.*
>
> And Adam gave names to all cattle, and to the fowl of the air and to every beast of the field; but for Adam there was not found a suitable helpmeet for him.
>
> And the LORD God *caused a deep sleep to fall upon Adam, and he slept*: and he took one of his ribs, and closed up the flesh instead thereof; and the rib, which the LORD God had taken from man, made he a woman, and brought her unto the man.
>
> And *Adam said*, "this is now bone of my bones, and flesh of my flesh: she shall be called Woman, because *she was taken out of Man.* Therefore shall a man leave his father and his mother, and shall cleave unto his wife: and they shall be one flesh."
>
> And they were *both naked*, the man and his wife, and *were not ashamed.* (KJV)

Before you get the wrong impression, God knew that Adam wasn't alone. The Spirit of God is always moving within and without our being as made self evident in Genesis 1:2 even if we refuse to acknowledge its existence. However, when we are unaware of our God self image and likeness, we *feel* a lot of things, most of which are false perceptions of our lower minds. Adam was a purely spiritual being—*from the beginning.* The fact that Adam forgot his true self image shouldn't surprise us—we all do!

Recall, if you will, what we discussed earlier regarding the growth and development phase of our life. Remember how we talked about the way in which we humans adopt certain beliefs and develop certain behaviors of our individual environments? We believe that the Genesis creation writers were trying to convey this growth and development phase of Adam's life.

What happened to Adam happens to all of us. Adam incurred *First IAM amnesia.* Adam became completely over-identified with his flesh (body) and overwhelmed by his material world—forgetting altogether his spiritual identity which was, in fact, his only identity. What's really fascinating about this particular part of the creation narrative is this: Adam's helpmeet was residing within himself all along; however, he failed to recognize it. But let's back up a minute.

Read Genesis 2:18-20 again. Notice that God declares that Adam shouldn't be alone and so he brings all the animals before Adam so as to see what Adam would call them? The text goes on to say that, "whatsoever Adam called every living creature that was the name thereof." This is a critical part of the Genesis creation narrative because Adam, back in Genesis 1:28, was given a great deal of power and authority. And let's not forget what Psalm 8:6-8 said, "Thou madest him to have dominion over the works of thy hands; thou hast put all things under his feet: All sheep and oxen, yea, and the beasts of the field; the fowl of the air, and the fish of the sea, and whatsoever passeth through the paths of the seas." But as we read the account of Genesis 2:23-24, Adam dooms himself by declaring his inner helpmeet to be merely *flesh and bone.* In another words,

Adam did exactly what Paul asserted in Romans 1:23, he "changed the glory of the incorruptible God into an image made like to corruptible man, and to birds, and four-footed beasts, and creeping things." Adam, without any contemplation or consideration, names God's image and likeness just as he had done with *the birds, four-footed beasts, and the creeping things* of the earth according to his flesh not his Spirit.

And before we decide to judge Adam for his error, aren't we doing the same when we call ourselves fat, ugly, and diseased or worse yet, when we call others those things? Is that what we really think of the image and likeness of God in our selves—in others? Don't you realize that when you call yourself stupid, inept, incapable, powerless, and the like, that you are calling the *incorruptible image of God* within you by the labels, titles, beliefs, and opinions of your *corruptible physical nature*? Your flesh is dying. Every day your flesh gets closer and closer to its material expiration date. Your lower flesh is corrupting and so are the elements of this earth.[48] So why are you putting your faith in a dying and decaying material image? If you'll allow the Spirit of God to transform your mind, your body and your earth will follow suit!

It appears that the real sin of Adam was poor self esteem, a departure from logic and reason. Thus, Adam's error didn't occur when his *helpmeet* fed him a piece of fruit from the Tree of the Knowledge of Good and Evil. The Tree of the Knowledge of Good and Evil was simply the result of Adam's natural evolution, because of his low self worth and false sense of pride. Adam's sin was subjecting and subordinating the incorruptible image of God to the corruptible image and likeness of his lower world and subsequent material self image.

When we have a poor self image, we have a greater propensity to be led by our fleshly lusts and desires—our lower minds. That's the weird thing about low self esteem; it leads to pride and reckless behavior whereas the image and likeness of God leads to humility and self

---

[48] 2 Peter 3:10

control. Adam was being led by his carnal and primitive minds rather than by his true identity which was his spirit. Again, Adam's true helpmeet was the Spirit of God within him. Unfortunately, Adam used his authority in a deadly and unaware way and called the incorruptible image of God corruptible by stating, " . . . this is now bone of my bones, and flesh of my flesh." Adam's *First IAM amnesia* cost him a life of abundance and peace. Adam was created with divine rights and authority; however, he chose a very different path for himself; a path he didn't have to travel.

Consequences of a Lower Self Image

The Genesis chapter two narrative demonstrates what a life lived outside of one's God image and likeness looks like. Listed below are the consequences of Adam's actions while abiding under the lower identities of the earth:

1. Adam's false and poor self image caused him to become over-identified with his flesh and material environment rather than live by his true God nature in Spirit. (Genesis 2:23 and 3:12)

When we don't know who we are in the *First IAM*, we become whatever somebody says we are. Many times the voices that we hear in our head are the words of our own self-deceived and depraved lower self or worse yet, the voices of other self-deceived individuals of our past. There is only one sure fire way to combat self-deception; to become aware of your true self image and likeness in Spirit. We cannot identify with our God self and our flesh and blood simultaneously.[49] The Christ says, "No man can serve two masters: for either he will hate the one, and love the other; or else he will hold to the one, and despise the other."[50] Our Master is One—God! We can know this One by becoming *First IAM* self aware!

---

[49] 1 Corinthians 15:50

[50] Matthew 6:24

2. Adam's false and poor self image caused him to fear and shame. (Genesis 3:7-10)

When we don't know who we are in the *First IAM*, we become fearful and overly anxious. Fear is the result of a lack of wisdom and discernment. Hosea 4:6 says, "My people are destroyed for a lack of knowledge." 1 John 4:18 says, "There is no fear in love; but perfect love casteth out fear: because fear hath torment. He that feareth is not made perfect in love." Fearful people create fearful institutions and societies. Fearful communication corrupts good beliefs and attitudes.[51] Corrupt beliefs and attitudes give rise to depraved behaviors. God has already declared all *very good*.[52] The self-deceived man has decided that he knows better than God; therefore, he has created a world of good versus evil, black versus white, normal versus abnormal, up versus down, right versus wrong, them versus us.

Once we become aware of our *First IAM* self image, we become aware of the knowledge of God. The knowledge and wisdom of God leads us into all truth.[53] It is this truth, the truth about who and what we really are, which sets us free from man's world of duality.[54] The *First IAM* identity liberates us from good versus evil, black versus white, normal versus abnormal, up versus down, right versus wrong, them versus us. Fear and shame are constructs of a people who know not their true God nature and identity.

You don't have to follow after the blind, deaf, and lame anymore! Becoming your *First IAM* self is becoming the child of God.[55] Being imbued with the *I AM* name and the spiritual likeness of God is a divine right; a right that no one can take from you![56]

---

51 1 Corinthians 15:33

52 Genesis 1:31

53 John 16:13

54 John 8:32

55 Romans 8:14

56 Romans 8:39

3. Adam's false and poor self image caused him to blame and place false value judgments on himself, God, others, and his world. Genesis 3:12

When we don't know who we are in the *First I AM*, we blame everyone else for our circumstances and failures—most especially God. We have no business placing value or passing judgment on anything, much less God and others. When you have no value in yourself—how can you assess the value of anything else or anyone else? You can't. Values require measurement. Man cannot measure the immeasurable. However, man can know the ways of God.

First Corinthians 2:11 says, " . . . no one discerns (comes to know and comprehend) the thoughts of God except the Spirit of God." When we fail to value the image and likeness of God within our very self, we lose our right to pass judgment and place value on anything or anyone else—most especially God. Because we don't know who and what we are, we blame others for our failed and fruitless lives; we become victims rather than victors. But how can we blame others for our errors? Aren't we all just victims creating more victims? We certainly are most especially when we continue to perpetuate the false doctrines, precepts, laws, and traditions of unconscious men and women. But we don't have to remain asleep.[57] We can be transformed through the renewing of our minds.[58] We can change our current *AM I* mindset to the *I AM* truth!

4. Adam's false and poor self image caused him to react according to the primitive parts of his brain which are always irrational, illogical, and rash. (Genesis 3:1, 12)

When we don't know who we are in the *First I AM,* we are driven by the lower regions of our brain. These lower regions do not think contemplatively, they respond emotionally and irrationally. To employ

57 1 Corinthians 15:51

58 Romans 12:2; Titus 3:5

the higher parts of our brain, those parts which think rationally and logically, take commitment, patience, and self mastery. These are pursuits which are imbued by the Spirit of God. The Spirit of God is our highest *helpmeet;* our highest mind.[59] The *First IAM* self image seeks after and focuses entirely on the higher things of God.[60] The *Higher Self Image* is centered in the Spirit; therefore all things are received with a balanced and sound mind. God is not a spirit of chaos but of light, peace, and order.[61] Find your *First IAM* self image and experience true peace and logic for your world!

5. Adam's false and poor self image caused him to perceive he lacked something as if God was withholding. (Genesis 3:5-6)

Again, when we don't know who we are in the *First IAM*, we place value judgments on God, ourselves, and others. We unfairly blame God for all our woes and ills. When we think negatively of God, it's a sure sign that we think negatively of our selves. Proverbs 6:31 says that a thief must repay seven-fold what he has stolen. That's a seven hundred percent return to those of us who have been robbed by life. Job knew who he was in God and was given twice as much as he had lost.[62] Many times, we are like Job's wife in that we would rather curse God and die than be like Job and believe God for full restoration and redemption—and live! The spiritual law of seven-fold can never be attained so long as we believe the worst about ourselves and more importantly, our God. We are of the belief that God allows the world to strip us of our worldly images and possessions so He can enforce the law of seven-fold. God wants to bless you—not hurt you! God wants to bless you beyond your wildest imagination. Whatever image of greatness you can conjure up in your small mind, God goes way beyond that image and more![63]

---

[59] 1 Corinthians 2:16; Hebrews 13:6

[60] Philippians 4:8

[61] Genesis 1:2-3; 1 Corinthians 14:33

[62] Job 42:8-10

[63] Ephesians 3:20

To know one's true self image and likeness is to know the true and living God. True salvation (wholeness of the mind, body, and soul) isn't achieved by a quick trip to the altar during the eleventh stanza of *Just as I am.* True salvation is all about eliminating the words "Just as" from our vocabulary and adopting the latter, *I AM,* with confidence! James 4:3 asserts that we have not because we do not ask for the right things. God is not slack in his promises toward us.[64] God isn't withholding anything from us. On the contrary, we are withholding things from God. In addition, we are withholding things from ourselves. When we deny ourselves the *First IAM* identity, we forfeit our divine rights to blessing, peace, wisdom, discernment, truth, power, authority, dominion, health, and abundant wealth. There were two trees in the garden of Eden; the Tree of the Knowledge of Good and Evil and the Tree of Life. Adam chose the tree of death over the Tree of Life.[65] Deuteronomy 30:19 says, "I call heaven and earth to record this day against you, that I have set before you life and death, blessing and cursing: therefore choose life that both thou and thy seed may live." We implore you to do the same, choose life by choosing to abide in your *First IAM* identity!

6. Adam's false and poor self image caused him to lose self control. (Genesis 3:6, 12)

When we don't know who we are in the *First IAM*, we lose control of our lives. Self mastery is a *higher self image* construct. We were given dominion and authority over our lives and our world.[66] When we lost sight of our *First IAM* image and likeness in God, we lost sight of our dominion and authority also. Those with a poor self concept find it difficult to control anything much less their appetites, health, and finances. America's economic and healthcare issues are the result of its collective poor self concept. America was supposedly founded upon Judeo-Christian beliefs. However, those beliefs were only as good as their source. Most of what we believe is the result of someone else's fear

64 2 Peter 3:9; 1 Corinthians 2:9

65 Genesis 2:17

66 Genesis 1:28

and shame which is due in part to their poor self concept. It appears that America needs a *First IAM* face lift if it plans on maintaining its preeminence in the world. It's not an impossible feat, you know. The temple of God is built one stone at a time. Each of us, operating within our true *First IAM* identity represents the stones of God's house.[67] Luke 19:37-40 puts it like this,

> And when he [Christ] was come nigh, even now at the descent of the mount of Olives, the whole multitude of the disciples began to rejoice and praise God with a loud voice for all the mighty works that they had seen; saying, Blessed be the King that cometh in the name of the Lord: peace in heaven, and glory in the highest. And some of the Pharisees from among the multitude said unto him, Master, rebuke thy disciples. And he answered and said unto them, I tell you that, if these should hold their peace, the stones would immediately cry out. (KJV)

Let us hold not our peace any longer! Let us become the precious stones of God's temple by becoming the *First IAM*; the image and likeness he has purposed for us to be before the foundation of the earth was set!

Our Children

We would be remiss if we didn't make a quick reference concerning the rearing of a child in today's climate and culture.

Proverbs 22:6 reads,

> Train up a child in the way he should go: and when he is old, he will not depart from it. (KJV)

We find the word *train* to be an excellent choice considering that our job as parents is to *coach* our children to become the best adults

[67] 1 Peter 2:9

that they can be for the purposes of God's overall divine plan. We believe that coaching a child in the way he/she should go, is extremely important. We also believe that by training a child in the precepts of the *First IAM* identity can very well mean the difference between that child choosing the life of Christ (*Him*) which leads to abundance and health or choosing the path of Adam (*them*) which leads to dis-ease and death.

Sadly, most of us have been reared under the fundamentalists and literalist interpretations of man's image and likeness. Unfortunately, that institution has failed to demonstrate man's true divine purpose; to reflect God's image and likeness in the earth! Through the training/coaching series of the *First IAM*® and the *IAM*Renewed4Life® programs, we wish to instruct all people in the ways of God so as to make them aware of their true nature. Not only do we wish for people to know their true nature and identity in Spirit, but we wish for them to understand how to live in that image and likeness so as to replenish the soul of man with joy, peace, and comfort.

By coaching our children in the way of their true identity, they will never experience the struggles that we adults have had to endure. Knowing their *First IAM* identity will ensure that they will never know another identity save God's. This knowledge and awareness in the child of today will indeed transform the world of tomorrow. Can you imagine it? We can. Therefore, the timeless truths that you learn from the *First IAM* coaching materials as an adult must be shared with your children. If you don't have a child, find one or several and teach this information to them. In this way, you will be fulfilling the mission of the *First IAM* which is to go into your individual universe and teach the Good News to those that are waiting!

Chapter 3

THE *FIRST IAM* HIGHER SELF MIND

We demonstrated in the last chapter what the *First IAM self image* represents. We stated that the *First IAM self image* is the *higher self image and likeness of God.* Now that we have a truer understanding of what the *First IAM self image* is all about, let's turn our attention to the *higher self mind* which is the *First IAM mind* of God. In this chapter we will examine the human brain so as to provide the student of Spirit with a better understanding and logical reasons for many of their own behaviors and the behaviors of others.

Reptiles Can and Do Speak!

According to Ken Ham, the author of the book, *Already Gone: Why Your Kids Will Quit Church and What You Can Do To Stop It,* stated that,

> "Sunday school syndrome" is contributing to the epidemic [of a mass exodus from religion] rather than helping alleviate it. Sunday school tends to focus on inspiration and morality of Bible stories, rather than how to defend the authority of the Bible. The "Bible stories" told in Sunday school are separated from "hard facts." As a result, children will turn to school books for facts and answers, instead of the Bible. *Already Gone* argues that if a child is unable to defend the historicity and fact of Genesis, then he or she will quickly be disillusioned with the church. "Ultimately, if we are unable to defend Genesis, we have allowed the enemy to

> attack our Christian faith and undermine the very first book of the Bible.[68]

Although we disagree with many of Ken Ham's beliefs regarding creationism and his interpretations of the Genesis creation narrative, we do agree that something has to be done to stop biblical illiteracy in our country—and our world.

Our beliefs are quite simple; reptiles can and do speak but not like we've been told by our Sunday school teachers. They speak to us through our genetics and our primitive prehistoric brain neural pathways. Although many of us fail to recognize or accept the process of evolution, it nevertheless exists and is made self-evident by our history, our blood, by our brains, and more importantly, by our actions.

For instance, our flight or fight mechanism is present because of our earliest ancestors. Some people wish to deny their animal evolution but the truth is our bodies (including our brains) are made up of the earth's elements. We also believe that the process of evolution is not only scientifically sound but also completely compatible with Scripture. For instance, in the Genesis chapter 1 narrative, the animals are created first—that is, before mankind. Mankind, in the Genesis chapter 2 narrative, is formed from the substance of the earth. Based upon the aforementioned biblical texts, mankind developing from earlier life forms isn't farfetched and certainly isn't disturbing. It is the ego of man which finds it difficult to believe that his physical body may have evolved from a lower life form; a life form with a lower intelligence. Nevertheless, the truth is, well, let's just put it this way—the proof is in the pudding.

Therefore, our goal is to find God's mind (which is Spirit) so as to lead our primitive brain and body to peace and abundance. Up until this moment, our environment has fashioned our brain—our thoughts,

---

[68] Ken Ham, *Already Gone: Why Your Kids Will Quit Church and What You Can Do To Stop It,* Green Forest AK, Master Books 2009, pg.37

ideas, beliefs, attitudes, and behaviors. The *First IAM®* program is interested in regenerating the memory of the brain to think in line with the true nature of Spirit.

The Triune Brain[69]

In the mid 1950s, the American physician and neuroscientist, Paul MacLean, formulated his triune brain hypothesis. MacLean theorized that through the evolutionary span of time, the human brain began to change and to develop into an increasingly complex system. A new brain formed over an older brain, until there were three very distinct brains, each performing and fulfilling its own specific tasks and purpose. While it is true that MacLean's triune brain model has been deemed too broad to be of value to students of neuroanatomy, we believe that Dr. MacLean's triune brain model has significant importance to the *First IAM* thesis. In fact, we believe that MacLean's findings provide us with tremendous insight into not only the physical evolution of the three brains of mankind but also his spiritual evolution. We believe that having a sound understanding of the triune brain model in its simplest form will provide the student of Spirit (*First IAM-er*) with many answers, as it pertains to the neuro-personal evolution of man.

Our goal in providing this intriguing information is to understand more fully why we do, say, and think in the ways we do, even though we wish to do, say, and think otherwise. In a nutshell, we wish to answer the question the apostle Paul posed in Romans 7:15-25 once and for all.

We also believe that Dr. MacLean's hypothesis was understood by the ancients who wrote the Genesis narrative thousands of years ago. It appears that the ancients were more spiritually attuned than we first believed or have been led to believe by fundamentalists and literalists. What we found most fascinating was the depth of their knowledge and wisdom regarding these physiological and psychological truths which,

[69] Paul MacLean, *The Triune Brain in Evolution*, Springer; 1st Edition, January 31, 1990

by the way, were not discovered by neuroscientists and paleontologists until recently.

The Garden of Eden and the Triune Mind of Man

Dr. MacLean believed that the brain was actually three distinct brains in one. Each of the three respective brains was developed successfully in response to the evolutionary need for survival. Each brain was designed to execute specific functions individually; however, all three can and do interact with one another on a regular basis. What's most interesting to us regarding this triune brain theory is its uncanny resemblance to the Genesis chapters 2 and 3 narratives. For instance, we observed that MacLean's reptilian lower brain had remarkable similarities to the function of the serpent personified in Genesis chapter 3, while the paleomammalian middle brain, resembled the actions of Eve. We also recognized the processes of the neocortex higher brain, which harmonizes quite well with Adam's purpose and divine design in Genesis chapters 1 and 2.

We believe that the Garden of Eden represents the *higher mind* of man that, when governed by the *First I AM higher self image,* can and does flourish and abides in a continual state of bliss (Paradise). We believe this integral part of man's higher brain (neocortex) may very well prove to be a God space which, if developed properly, can prove to be man's saving grace!

Anatomy of the Triune Brain Model

Without getting too deep into the anatomy and physiology of the brain, we will attempt to give a brief overview of Paul MacLean's triune brain theory.

The Reptilian Brain—"R-Complex"

According to Dr. Paul MacLean, the reptilian complex of the human brain is thought to be the oldest and most primitive brain-layer of mankind. It's also known as the *R-complex,* the *lower brain,* and the *reptilian brain.* The name *reptilian brain* was derived from the idea that the forebrains of prehistoric reptiles and birds were dominated by these same structures; namely, the brain stem and the cerebellum. It's important for the purposes of our study that the student of Spirit understands the function of the reptilian brain.

The brain stem and cerebellum (the reptilian brain complex) control the instinctual survival drives and behaviors of a species. This complex controls muscle coordination, balance, and autonomic functions such as breathing and heart beat regulation. It is, therefore, extremely reactive to stimuli and reacts to stimuli automatically without conscious thought; it functions in habitual patterns, finding it nearly impossible to alter its primitive learned survival instincts. There is nothing emotional about this region of the brain. Like the snake, it is cold and calculating. However, it can and does interact with the emotional brain, the paleomammalian middle brain.

MacLean believed that the reptilian brain evolved during the Triassic period (from 248 to 206 million years ago).[70] It evolved as a helpmeet for man's survival. This brain gives rise to what is commonly termed the Four Fs (e.g. feeding, fighting, fleeing, and fornicating). It regulates our fight-or-flight response, controls our body's temperature, digestion, reproduction, and our hunger. Its over arching goal is to keep you alive and to multiply your genes in the earth. Thus, many of its behaviors are animalistic in nature. It performs many of its function based upon external triggers (stimuli); triggers that cause a programmed response. Some of the traits associated with the reptilian brain are aggression, social dominance, seeking a mate, sexual rigidity, obsessive-compulsive behaviors and practices, ritualistic practices, fear and anxiety, fearful submission, and greed.

These basic functions controlled by the higher brain (neocortex) help to encourage our more highly evolved thoughts and beliefs. When the

---

70 http://thewholepictureofhealth.blogspot.com/2010/05/brain-function-behavior-and-emotions.html (accessed May 8, 2010)

base instinctual part of our brain is subdued and controlled healthily, it frees us to think contemplatively about new, wise, and safer ways to accomplish our God-given goals and purposes for our lives. It frees us to find better ways to create unity and cohesiveness with our fellow neighbor without the fear of extinction.

God on the Brain

In his book, *How God Changes Your Brain,*[71] neuroscientist Andrew Newberg discovered that when an individual contemplates God long enough, extraordinary things occur in the brain; the neural functioning of the brain actually begins to change. We find Dr. Newberg's findings to be compatible with Scripture.

Hebrews 4:12 says,

> For the word of God is quick, and powerful, and sharper than any two-edged sword, piercing even to the dividing asunder of soul and spirit, and of the joints and marrow, and is a discerner of the thoughts and intents of the heart. (KJV)

First Samuel 10:9 asserts,

> The Spirit of the LORD will come upon you in power, and you will prophesy with them; and *you will be changed into a different person.* (NIV)

Dr. Newberg describes these brain changes when he writes,

> Different circuits become activated, while others become deactivated. New dendrites are formed, new synaptic connections are made, and the brain becomes more sensitive to subtle realms of experience. Perceptions alter, beliefs begin

71 Andrew Newberg, *How God Changes the Brain*, New York, Ballantine Books March 24, 2009

> to change, and if God has meaning for you, then God becomes neurologically real.[72]

By becoming more familiar with the most primitive part of our brain, we become more aware of our behaviors—behaviors that lead to unsatisfying results and consequences, more times than not. This can literally transform our thinking and our responses to specific life stressors or perceived threats to our self-rule. We agree with Dr. Newberg's findings regarding changes within the neurological pathways of the brain when the mind remains focused if stayed on the *higher* things of God.[73] The *First IAM higher mind* can ease the fears of the lower reptilian mind and over time can curtail its reaction time to perceived threats.

Venom or Anti-Venom?

James 1:18 says that we are to be swift to hear, slow to speak, and slow to wrath. The only way to heed the teacher's words of wisdom is to employ the *higher mind of God.* James 4:8 says that if we draw closer to God, he will draw closer to us. We cannot afford to remove God from our everyday lives. The effects of our lower *self-un-awareness* is killing us, just as Genesis 2:17 warned us it would. It's time for a new approach to the creation narrative of Genesis. It's time for us to grow up and think right!

In Genesis chapter 3, we are introduced to an excellent personification of our most primitive mind. Genesis 3:1 reads,

> Now the serpent was more subtil than any beast of the field which the LORD God had made. (KJV)

Notice that the writer employs the word, *subtil.* The word *subtil* in the Hebrew is the word *'aruwm.* It means to be cautious, prudent, and

---

72 Andrew Newberg, *How God Changes the Brain*, New York, Ballantine Books March 24, 2009

73 Philippians 4:8

perceptive. Why do you suppose that God created our reptilian brains to be cautious, prudent, and perceptive? God created our reptilian brains for our survival—plain and simple. In the beginning of our evolutionary process, if we were going to survive the threats of a dangerous world, we would need a cautious, prudent, and perceptive mechanism. Remember, God created everything and deemed it very good and the reptilian brain is no exception.[74] It is this brain which kept us thriving, multiplying, and replenishing the earth!

As we demonstrated earlier, the reptilian brain is made up of the brain stem and the cerebellum. We humans cannot survive without a functioning brain stem. Not only does our brain stem provide us with the ability to breathe automatically, it regulates our circulation and digestion. The cerebellum, on the other hand, is responsible for our balance, movement, and coordination. The reptilian brain is what enables us to fight a predator or flee for safety. In addition, it controls our sexual drives. Without a sexual drive, we wouldn't be able to fulfill the mandate of Genesis 1:28—to be fruitful and to multiply.

However, too much of even a *very good* thing can prove to be unhealthy and disastrous for us and our world. Thus, what was once our means of survival could prove to be a thing that could also kill us. Interestingly enough, snake venom is the one thing that can cure a snake bite. It appears that we need to become more familiar with the thing that can both kill us and cure us if we are to survive for another 14 billion years.

For instance, external occurrences have the potential to change our behavior and thought patterns in unhealthy ways if we are not vigilant about our thought-life. Many times environmental triggers stir up the aggressive, ritualistic, and fear-based type behaviors of the serpent-like lower brain while other external triggers employ the limbic system (the emotional brain), giving rise to old primitive feelings and memories.

---

[74] Genesis 1:31

It's important to understand that your animal-like lower brains make instinctual automatic decisions and react without your consciousness. This is why 1 Peter 5:8 says, "Be sober, be vigilant; because *your adversary* the devil, as a roaring lion, walketh about, seeking whom he may devour."

Our lower minds definitely move as 1 Peter 5:8 asserts, however, we can allow our lower brains to operate naturally without giving up our dominion or our authority over our thoughts and behaviors.

Once we learn to maintain balance between the *higher mind* and the lower minds, we will be able to live as Isaiah 11:6 asserts, "The wolf shall dwell with the lamb, and the leopard shall lie down with the kid; and the calf and the young lion and the fatling together; and a little child shall lead them." Becoming aware of one's *First IAM higher self image* will help attain the mental balance that is necessary for a successful and healthy life. The *First IAM higher self image* helps us to self-regulate the emotions and thoughts of our lower brains with compassion and optimism.

The Paleomammalian Brain—"Limbic System"

The paleomammalian brain (mid-brain), or as it was called by MacLean, the limbic system, processes emotions and makes split second decisions based on patterns of information previously received in the early stages of brain development.

The hippocampus (a major component of the limbic system), on the other hand, operates the conversion of incoming information from short-term memory to long-term memory, and is necessary for the recall of that memory.

Research has demonstrated that repeated use of the neural pathways of the hippocampus enhances our memory storage. Dr. Candace Pert believes that the hippocampus helps to select specific memories by attaching an *emotional marker* (chemical messengers) to the event so that they are recalled with ease.[75] Memories are made because of an associated emotionally charged (e.g., first date, prom night, wedding day, tonsillectomy) event. This also explains why we remember certain words that have been spoken to us. This is why words are so very powerful—they are emotionally charged and it's that emotional energy that creates a memory in our brain—good, bad, or indifferent.

Dr. Pert says that because the amygdala arouses feelings; damage to the amygdala can eradicate emotionally-charged memories ("molecules of emotion"). Since we are driven by pleasure and were created for pleasure, we need the amygdala to counter balance the needs of the lower reptilian brain. Again, the amygdala links emotions with actions. This, in turn, helps to inhibit the lower brain's instincts, which can often prove to be unhealthy or impractical if not monitored closely. For instance, the limbic system regulates our primal instincts such as sex and hunger in a way that makes us better able to derive pleasure from satisfying these instincts. The limbic system also helps us refrain from behaviors or activities that create pain or discomfort in order to protect the body from danger and harm. We will have a greater tendency to repeat an action or behavior if the experience proves to be pleasurable. The opposite of that is also true: painful experiences are usually avoided. Therefore, we need both our lower and our middle brains for a fulfilling, safe, and pleasurable life.

It is amazing how many decisions are made using the limbic system brain. Most people make life choices based upon their emotions rather than their logic and reason. Sadly, many of us are completely unaware that our middle and lower brains are acting, reacting, deciding, and filtering incoming stimuli and information. This explains how we can be ranting and raving one minute and completely rational and apologetic the next. This demonstrates how our limbic and reptilian brains can be activated while our neocortical brain remains the ever watchful observer. Unfortunately, our logical brain doesn't usually come

---

75 Candace Pert, *Measuring the Immeasurable*, 17, 21, Boulder CO, Sounds True, Inc., 2008

to our rescue until after we have made complete fools of ourselves and have said things we wish could take back. Luckily for our generation, we have neuroscience on our side, and with the right information and self awareness; we can change the outcome of any given situation or life choice!

In Genesis 2:21-23 we are formerly introduced to the limbic system of our brain.

> God caused a deep sleep to fall upon Adam, and he slept: and he took one of his ribs, and closed up the flesh instead thereof; And the rib, which the LORD God had taken from man, made he a woman, and brought her unto the man. And Adam said, This is now bone of my bones, and flesh of my flesh: she shall be called Woman, because she was taken out of Man. (KJV)

We suppose you're asking the question, What on earth does Genesis 2:21-23 have to do with our middle brain? We're glad you asked. We wish to demonstrate the mind-body connection. Dr. Eva Mezey and her colleagues of the National Institutes of Health proved conclusively that there is indeed a mind-body connection. Dr. Mezey found that transplanted bone marrow cells can turn into new brain cells.[76] Dr. Candace Pert had this to say regarding Dr. Mezey's remarkable research:

> Stem cells—cells that are undifferentiated and have yet to become organ cells—are made in the bone marrow which we already knew. We also knew that stem cells move through the blood to other systems and organs. But the news that they move out of the bone marrow, eventually becoming neurons in the nervous system, was shocking. Dr. Mezey found this migration happening not only in response to illness, as when stem cells grew into immune cells, but as a matter of course. And even more shocking was that these stem

[76] Journal Article, Samson, Kurt, *Transplanted Bone Marrow Cells Migrate, Become Neurons, Neurology Today* 3, no. 7 (July 2003): 18, 21

> cells weren't just showing up in the spinal cord (which I consider an extension of the brain), but also in the highest part of the brain, a structure known as the "frontal cortex." **The bones are giving rise to the brain!** Ancient Chinese medicine says that chi, loosely translated as "the life force," originates in the bone."[77]

Now, let's reexamine the earlier Genesis text again in light of Dr. Pert's and Dr. Mezey's findings.

> God caused a deep sleep to fall upon Adam, and he slept: and he took one of his ribs, and closed up the flesh instead thereof; And the rib, which the LORD God had taken from man, made he a woman, and brought her unto the man. And Adam said, this is now *bone of my bones, and flesh of my flesh*: she shall be called Woman, because she was taken out of Man. (KJV)

Hebrews 4:12 says,

> For the word of God is quick, and powerful, and sharper than any two-edged sword, piercing even to the dividing asunder of soul and spirit, and *of the joints and marrow*, and is *a discerner of the thoughts and intents of the heart.* (KJV)

Here's the bottom line, our mind and body have a positive physiological and neurological bi-directional effect on one another; a fact verified scripturally and scientifically. The actions of Adam (Neocortex "rational" brain) had a direct effect on Eve (Limbic middle "emotional" brain), and vice versa. Unfortunately, the serpent (Reptilian lower "primitive" brain) had a greater influence on Eve than Adam. But why? Awareness, that's why. Adam was in a deep sleep—he lost sight of his *First I AM higher self image.* If we are going to be successful at taking dominion and authority over our lives, we each need an aware Adamic (Christ "higher") brain to balance our lower two.

---

77 Candace Pert, *Measuring the Immeasurable*, 20-21, Boulder, CO, Sounds True, Inc., 2008

The Neomammalian Brain—"Neocortex"

Now for the good news! The Neocortex is the newest and most sophisticated part of the brain. This is the region of the brain where you think about thinking. It controls the higher levels of cognition such as logic, rationale, reason, creativity, language and the integration of sensory information. Unfortunately, just as we demonstrated earlier, the neocortex (the unaware Adam) can be overpowered (hijacked) by the brains beneath it, most especially the limbic brain (desire and the emotionally charged Eve).

For instance, an old memory which was attached to a fearful emotion as a child can jump start the amygdala region of the brain when confronted with an event (trigger) that resembles the earlier memory. This response can override the higher brain, sending all sorts of chemicals and urgent signals throughout the body—telling the body to prepare for danger. The brain then frantically searches itself for relevant responses to the threat, taking complete control of the neurological and physiological wheel. In some cases, the brain tells the body to run, flee, or fight, circumventing logical, rational, and reasonable thinking skills altogether. This type of response is a wonderful mechanism created by God to save our lives. However, when this type of response is employed regularly because of chronic stress and anxiety, it can cause serious physiological issues for the body and the brain, creating a very toxic internal environment—not to mention its potential to hinder our careers, our marriages, and our relationships severely.

Hence, the lack of neocortical authority/dominance can cause us to act/react in irrational and unreasonable ways. Individuals who lack coping skills fall into this dangerous cycle of limbic and reptilian usurpation. This type of behavioral response to non life-threatening stressors can hold a person hostage to unreal and unsubstantiated fears and that's certainly no way to live.

You need to understand that your middle and lower brains don't know the difference between a real life-threatening event from a non life-threatening event. In addition, your middle and lower brains don't know that you have no coping skills and frankly don't care. The neocortex, on the other hand, does care, but again, it finds itself rendered powerless and usurped by the lower brains on a regular basis, so how much help can it really be to us? The only hope for the neocortex and our lower brains is the intercession of the aware prefrontal cortex. The prefrontal cortex allows abstract thought and reasoning to occur. And while this sounds like great news, there is a caveat: we have to allow this part of the brain to do its effectual work by becoming aware of its presence.

The Prefrontal Cortex—"PFC"

Just as there was a fourth man in the fiery furnace of Daniel 3:25, there appears to be a fourth aspect of the neocortex which neuroscience has paid significant attention to these days: the prefrontal cortex. The prefrontal cortex (PFC) appears to be the missing link as it pertains to the balance of the triune brain mental processes. The PFC is responsible for the psychological executive function of the brain.[78] Its job is to differentiate between conflicting thoughts, determine good and bad, better and best, same and different, future consequences of current activities, working toward a defined goal, prediction of outcomes, expectation based on actions, and social "control", meaning the ability to suppress urges that, if not suppressed, could lead to socially-unacceptable outcomes.[79]

These executive functions sound a lot like the effectual work of the Christ mind and/or mind of the Spirit. Could it be that the prefrontal cortex is the seat of spiritual enlightenment? According to neurologist, Dr. David Perlmutter, our prefrontal cortex—our fourth brain, as he terms it—is in fact our link to enlightenment. Dr. Perlmutter believes that the synergy between the PFC and the lower brains took several generations to develop; however, it did happen. Dr. Perlmutter poses

78 "Prefrontal Cortex," *Wikipedia, the Free Encyclopedia*, http://en.wikipedia.org/wiki/Prefrontal_cortex (accessed 4/8/2011

79 "Prefrontal Cortex," *Wikipedia, the Free Encyclopedia*, http://en.wikipedia.org/wiki/Prefrontal_cortex (accessed 4/8/2011

an interesting question regarding the evolutionary process of the higher mind and self consciousness in his book, *Power Up Your Brain, the Neuroscience of Enlightenment.* He writes:

> In the scheme of history, the quest for metaphysical answers about the origin of life died when Charles Darwin published *The Origin of Species.* The popular understanding of the time was that life is a perennial struggle for survival, that humankind is governed by a harsh law of the jungle where only the fittest win. But, fortunately, after centuries of scientists' dismissal and ignoring of the ancient teachings, people in all walks of life are once again asking the mystic's questions about the significance and potential of human consciousness. Could evolution have also been favoring the survival of the wisest?[80]

Based upon the significant numbers of those who are leaving the faith of their youth, we believe that history has proven Dr. Perlmutter correct in his supposition regarding the *survival of the wisest.* The history of human consciousness demonstrates a tremendous struggle to overcome its base instinctual fears (lower brains) as it pertains to God and self (higher mind). There does seem to be a distinct difference between the way we *used* to think (older awareness) versus the way we think today (newer awareness), most especially as it pertains to our empathy, compassion, and tolerance of other beliefs and religious traditions.

For example, the God of our youth is certainly more oppressive and authoritarian than the loving and all-inclusive God of our mid-life. We believe this newer awareness is what today's eighteen to thirty-year-olds are in search of, rather than the old tyrannical and intolerant beliefs of their grandparents. We also believe that the *First IAM* philosophy offers young people and older people alike, their faith, their Bible, and the use of their *higher mind* (PFC) without conflict.

---

80 Dr. David Perlmutter, M.D., F.A.C.N. and Alberto Villoldo, PhD *Power Up Your Brain, the Neuroscience of Enlightenment*, 24, Hay House, Inc. 1st Edition February 2011, United States

Mind Renewal

Romans 12:2 says,

> Be not conformed to this world: but be ye transformed by the renewing of your mind, that ye may prove what is that good, and acceptable, and perfect, will of God. (KJV)

The word *transformed* is the Greek word, *metamorphoo* meaning *to be changed into another form*; like a caterpillar is changed and transformed into a butterfly. The word *renewing* is the Greek word, *anakainosis. Anakainosis* comes from the root word, *anakainoo,* meaning *to be changed into a new and renovated kind of life; a better life.*

Paul is exhorting his students to undergo a tremendous change. Paul understands that metamorphosis cannot occur without mind regeneration. In another words, Paul knows that we have to think anew—we have to think differently.

Being conformed to the value systems and judgments of this world is fruitless and deadly, as is made evident in Genesis chapter 3. And frankly, we don't have to live by the earth's economy, for God has given us humans something extraordinarily special, something that no other species possesses. God has given us a *higher mind*—an anointed mind. With this mind we can control our lower minds and our individual universes which were always meant to be under our authority and dominion.

Don't misunderstand our position regarding worldly conformity. An individual can abstain from all sorts of worldly type behaviors, however, those types of changes alone are not enough to transform or regenerate one's mind. Remember, ritual type activities (exercise, dietary, and religious routines and practices) are functions of the lower minds and do not require higher mind oversight per se. True mind renewal comes as a result of true deliberate intention; making a concerted effort to think about thinking before acting or reacting. Of course this type of thinking or self consciousness requires a great deal of patience and effort. Nevertheless, the dividends are tremendous. For instance, Paul goes onto to say that by thinking about thinking (mind renewal); one can attain the good, perfect, and acceptable will of God for their lives.

Ephesians 4:23-24 says,

> Be renewed in the *spirit of your mind*; and that ye put on *the new man*, which *after God* is created in righteousness and true holiness. (KJV)

Here we are again; Paul asserts that the *First IAM* man is created after the image and likeness of God (Gen. 1:27a). In addition, Paul states that we are to be *renewed in the spirit* of our mind. What does it mean to be renewed in the spirit of our mind? The word *spirit* is the Greek word, *pneuma*. One of *Strong's Lexicon* definitions for this word is *the rational spirit, the power by which the human being feels, thinks, and decides.*[81] Your mind possesses an energy and a power—a spirit. Your brain is highly charged energetically. Your brain has the ability, power, and authority to transform your world! By thinking about thinking, you can literally transform your mind, body, and life within a relatively short period of time!

However, you will never experience your God-given power and authority so long as you refuse to *put on the new man*; the image and likeness of God—which is Spirit! There is one common theme of Paul's epistles; the *new man*—the *First IAM* man—the *higher self image and likeness of God!* Paul expends an enormous amount of energy and passion doing everything he can to lead his students into all truth regarding their true nature—their true God image and identity.

Titus 3:4-5 says,

> But then God our Savior showed us his kindness and love. He made us whole, not because of the good things we did, but because

[81] "Spirit" Strong's Lexicon #4151

> of his mercy. By the washing of regeneration and renewing of the Holy Spirit he gave us a new life. (NLT)

Again, simple ritualistic acts of abstinence don't create a renewed and regenerated mind—it simply creates a ritualistic lifestyle. The Spirit of God on the other hand, creates in us a new thought-life! If you *think* that you can begin *thinking* consciously without the effectual assistance and leadership of God—you are seriously mistaken. Remember, the lower minds are the base and instinctual minds of the earth; created to keep you alive and provide your life with the ability to experience pleasure rather than pain—period! Your *higher mind,* however, was created to do the good, perfect, and acceptable will of God. God is your *higher mind* and it's God's mind that will accomplish his design in your life![82] As Paul says in Philippians 2:5 and 3:15, let this mind be in you at all times!

God created all things in the heavens and in the earth. God deemed all things *very good.*[83] God created our reptilian and limbic brains for a perfectly good reason; for our survival and pleasure as we have clearly demonstrated. However, as we have also demonstrated, our lower brains are not suitable helpmeets when left alone—just as the serpent and Eve proved in Genesis chapter 3.

God has given us a *higher mind*—the mind of Christ, the mind of Spirit and truth—as a *suitable helpmeet.* The lower minds are of the flesh and earth whereas the *higher mind* is of the Spirit and heaven. The lower minds *mind* the things of the flesh and the earth whereas the *higher mind* minds the things of the Spirit and of heaven. Part of minding the things of Spirit is cultivating our *higher mind*—our *First I AM mind*—our God image and likeness.

We are to watch over, tend, cultivate, and care for Gods garden. God's garden is our physical brain. Maintaining our brain health is our highest

82 Isaiah 55:11

83 Genesis 1:31

calling. Our brain is where God walks and calls out to us in the still of the night and during the hustle and bustle of our busy day. God's voice is the voice of truth and wisdom. Learning to still the lower minds long enough to hear this voice of reason and wisdom should be our primary goal.

Wisdom is imparted via an aware and conscious mind. However, wisdom cannot penetrate a mind which is unhealthy, damaged, and non-responsive to God's words of truth. According to neuroscience, we humans use very little of our brains, but when we do, most of the stuff we think about are unreal thoughts—"what-if" thoughts—which create strongholds in our mind and our body. These false messages that we allow to circulate throughout our minds are procreating other memories which work against us rather than for us. In fact, these memories are so powerful that they block all other higher thoughts—good and positive God thoughts.

For the better part of our lives we allow our emotional brain (Eve) and our primitive reptilian brain (serpent), to usurp our mind of reason (neocortical brain—Adam) just like the narrative of Genesis chapter 3 illustrates. When we bow to the primal instincts of the reptilian brain and the irrational and illogical perceptions of the emotional brain, we yield the *First IAM* image and likeness of God also.

The spiritual wisdom weigh station of the prefrontal cortex (PFC) could have saved Adam from believing a lie about God's generosity and provision. Instead, Adam believed the lie and began to fear, which in turn begat his self-loathing and shame. It appears that Adam, after he had come down off of his biochemical overdose, regained his rational and logical mind, and thus came to his senses. So as you can see, when logic and reason are employed, rather than fear and shame, the truth—which has the power to make one free—is available. This is made evident from our Bible—most especially our Bible. In this way, we can use the Scriptures to understand ourselves, our God, and our world in order to live in unity with all things, because at the end of the day, it's all very good, as long as we are observing it all with the God part of our brains. It is apparent, from the latest statistics regarding obesity and the state of our nation's economy, that denial and walking through life on auto pilot are not conducive to a whole and healthy society. It takes an aware mind to become whole and sound. Adam's sleep cost him his life of abundance. Are we greater than Adam?

Fundamentalism doesn't encourage its adherents to be mindful. It asks them to follow blindly the precepts of the denomination's council rather than be led by the mind of the Spirit. As a matter of scientific fact, fundamentalism is fueled by the lower brains without an aware higher mind to illumine the deep and spiritual things of God.

While it seems plausible to us that Paul, *the apostle*, had no formal training in the discipline of neuroscience, he certainly understood the triune brain model of Paul, *the neuroscientist.* Armed with this new knowledge, we can begin to rebuild our faith in a logical and rational way that will not only transform our individual worlds, but help change the world at large! This is our prayer and ever-present objective!

The image and likeness cannot abide by the traditions of men for long. There is a change in consciousness coming very soon—it's been nearing its revelation for some time now. Make no mistake, it is coming—that's for sure! Are you ready? Will you recognize it or sense its presence when it does? Look up, for your redemption is closer than your lower brains think!

Chapter 4

THE *FIRST IAM* HIGHER SELF BODY

In the last chapter, we introduced the *First IAM higher self mind*—the *divine mind of God.* We discovered that mankind has three brains in one, and that reptiles can and do speak if we are willing to listen. We also discovered that how we govern our three brains can mean the difference between unity and disunity, bliss and misery, joy and sadness, peace and confusion, life and death. We demonstrated that when our three brains are influenced and controlled by the *First IAM higher self image* and *mind,* our *higher life* can and does flourish in a continual state of paradise. Now let's turn our attention to the *First IAM higher self body.*

Body Image

What is your body saying to you? Your body speaks, that's for sure, but your true body image is not the voice you're hearing when you hear things like *you're fat, you're never gonna be a size six or weigh 125 pounds or wear your skinny jeans ever again.* Those voices are the sounds of a negative world rooted in the regions of your lower and emotional minds.

Body image is simply one's perception of their personal and societal attractiveness. Our world, since the beginning of time, has placed a great deal of false value and judgment on the human anatomy. However, a person's false perceptions about the human body are not at all congruent with God's word.

Psalm 139:13-14 says,

> You made all the delicate, inner parts of my body and knit me together in my mother's womb. Thank you for making me so wonderfully complex! Your workmanship is marvelous—how well I know it. (NLT)

So what's the truth? What's your truth? Sure, we could all do a better job at our diet and exercise, and we certainly could change our habitual practices which certainly don't lend themselves to our highest good, but are we that far off the mark? Have we wandered so far off the path of health and fitness that we can't come back? Have the media and our society ruined our self concept beyond all hope?

We believe you can change your body image with very little effort! We believe this because we have done it ourselves! Most weight management and body image issues are between our two ears. The number on the scale isn't reality or at least it doesn't have to be. And the image in the mirror doesn't have to look like Nicole Richie or Arnold Schwarzenegger. Your body image is not the real you! The real you doesn't even have a body and the sooner your lower minds are introduced to the real you, the sooner your true body will resurrect.

Metamorphosis is not just a transformation of the external image, it's a change of the internal eye as well. We have to begin to *see* and *perceive* ourselves from a completely different viewpoint if we are going to transform into our *true body*. Our *true self* is timeless, formless, changeless, and eternal! Our physical body is simply a vehicle for our *true self image*. Within each individual body is a lean, mean, spiritual fighting machine! We need only to follow our God-given internal compass to find our way back to health and wholeness.

The famous artist, Michelangelo, had this to say about his own internal compass:

> In every block of marble I see a statue as plain as though it stood before me, shaped and perfect in attitude and action. I have only to hew away the rough walls that imprison the lovely apparition to reveal it to the other eyes as mine see it.[84]

What a beautiful depiction of one's vision and passion for artistic expression and what an excellent description of the work that God does regarding our true self image and likeness. We have to allow God to chisel away the *rough walls that imprison* the *lovely apparition of God* in us, a barrier created by our lower irrational minds and environment.

By ever increasing the wisdom and confidence of our *higher self mind* and our *higher self image*, we can at last reveal the true vision of our *highest self body*. This change occurs when we begin to eat for rational reasons rather than emotionally. We learn that our last meal is, in fact, not our last meal, and that portion control and moderation are our best friends, not false friends like flour, sugar, and processed foods.

Jeremiah 18:1-6 says,

> THE WORD which came to Jeremiah from the Lord: Arise and go down to the potter's house, and there I will cause you to hear My words. Then I went down to the potter's house, and behold, he was working at the wheel. And the vessel that he was making from clay was spoiled in the hand of the potter; so he made it over, reworking it into another vessel as it seemed good to the potter to make it. Then the word of the Lord came to me: O house of Israel, can I not do with you as this potter does? says the Lord. Behold, as the clay is in the potter's hand, so are you in My hand, O house of Israel. (AMP)

---

84 "Michelangelo Quotes," http://www.michelangelo-gallery.com/quotes.aspx (accessed June 2010)

God formed our bodies out of the elements of the earth; however, as we mature psychologically and spiritually, he begins to con-form us into the image of his only begotten—our spiritual *higher self, mind,* and *body.*

Yes, it's true that our initial image and likeness is formed by our environment, but it doesn't have to remain that way. Eventually, if we trust the God in us, we are reworked into our former image and likeness, which is Spirit. While it is true that your physical body looks just like those of your parents and genetic ancestors, your true self image looks just like God! If you think otherwise, you have been lied to. You are perfect! You are beautiful! You are the image and likeness of God! If you don't believe these things, you are listening to false friends and false voices!

Romans 9:20b says,

> Will what is formed say to him that formed it, why have you made me thus? (KJV)

We have to stop loathing our bodies and start treating them like our best friends. If you knew what your body was capable of affording you, you would treat it more gently and kindly, and would stop questioning God's handiwork. Your body is the temple of the greatest power in the universe. That power has the ability to take you places you've only dreamed of going. With the *right mind* and the *right self image*, you can transform not only your body, but your entire world!

Ephesians 3:20 says,

> God can do anything, you know—far more than you could ever imagine or guess or request in your wildest dreams! He does it not by pushing us around but by working within us, his Spirit deeply and gently within us. (MSG)

Your body is a super-natural vehicle—used of God for his pleasure and purpose! God's very Spirit is within your mortal body just waiting to come forth! A sick and depressed body cannot begin to live a life designed by God according to Ephesians 3:20.

The famous psychiatrist, Carl Jung, once said, "I'd rather be whole than good." Dr. Jung's comment reminds us of a story told in the Gospel of John. The Christ comes upon an impotent man lying near the pool of Bethesda. We are told that this man had been sick for thirty-eight years. When Jesus sees the man he approaches him and asks, "Wilt thou be made whole?" Notice Jesus didn't ask him if he wanted a new body or new legs, he asked him if he wanted to be made whole.

What does it mean to be whole? The Encarta Dictionary gives this definition for the word whole: *to be complete, including all parts or aspects, with nothing left out; not divided into parts or not regarded as consisting of separate parts*. Wow! That's exactly how God sees us—already!

God's Word Says We Are Complete

Genesis 2:1 says,

> So the creation of the heavens and the earth and everything in them was complete. (NLT)

Ephesians 3:19 says,

> You are made complete with all the fullness of life and power that comes from God. (NLT)

Colossians 2:10 says,

> Ye are complete in him [Christ], which is the head of all principality and power. (KJV)

God's Word Says We Are One with Spirit

First Thessalonians 5:23 says,

> May God himself, the God who makes everything holy and whole, make you holy and whole, put you together—spirit, soul, and body—and keep you fit . . . (MSG)

James 2:26 says,

> The very moment you separate body and spirit, you end up with a corpse. (MSG)

Ephesians 4:4 says,

> You were all called to travel on the same road and in the same direction, so stay together, both outwardly and inwardly. You have one Master, one faith, one baptism, one God and Father of all, who rules over all, works through all, and is present in all. Everything you are and think and do is permeated with Oneness. (MSG)

Do you want to be made whole—really whole? Are you more concerned with being good, being pretty, being thin, being anything other than being whole and one with God?

The Voice of God

Diets fail and the health care system is in crisis because people don't understand the true purpose for their body. However, there is good news: our bodies speak, and not only do they speak, they speak the language of God and his perfect design for our lives.

The face of medicine is rapidly changing as we write these words. This is an exciting time to be alive. We are moving beyond the origins of life and how it all began to an understanding of how energy fields are shaping and directing life. More specifically, scientists are trying to understand what makes a cell turn itself into a specific kind of cell that forms an organ or another kind of cell. The "experts" are trying to decode the code of life and thereby determine, at last, the source of life's information and hidden intelligence.

Our bodies are made up of innumerable and immeasurable amounts of chemical processes that create enzymes and proteins as well as the hormones and other substances that our bodies need in order to function properly. These processes are carefully orchestrated and conducted with an uncanny, exact precision. How these processes are choreographed is the subject and interest of some great scientific minds. The consensus at present is that there appears to be an invisible intelligence conducting the intricacies of life at the smallest level of life—the human cell.

It is truly amazing how something as tiny as the human cell can exert so much energy and power. Without cells, there would be no life. Each cell is crammed with tiny structures which aid in the thousands of processes that create and sustain our life. Each cell is truly like a universe within the universe—tiny factories of metabolism, the life sustaining chemical activity needed to convert energy.

With the advent of radiology and with the help of modern science, scientists are now able to see the detailed shapes of the individual kinds of molecules that perform the tasks of cellular life. Scientists have been discovering highly advanced operating systems in the cell that act essentially like computer programs. These operating systems are no less than marvelously perfect and insanely precise. To be perfectly honest, the human cell boggles the greatest minds of modern science.

The more we discover about these highly intelligent operating systems within the basic structures of life, the greater our curiosity becomes regarding the designer and controller of these very sophisticated systems. It appears that the kingdom of God is truly within us and the more we acquaint ourselves with this exquisite intelligence, the greater our wisdom and power to co-create our universe increases!

The Voice of the Earth

When we treat our bodies in a manner incongruent with God's perfect design, internal conflict occurs. Each of us feels the negative effects of our poor eating habits and lifestyle choices. We work too hard and relax too little. Eventually, we pay the ultimate price in our health. The symptoms of illness are the promptings of God. They are signs given to us from the universe to warn us that something is inconsistent with God's divine plan for our life.

Genesis 4:10 reads,

> . . . the voice of thy brother's blood crieth unto me from the ground. (KJV)

The earth has a voice. You are made of both earth and spirit. When your material body (clay), is dysfunctional or dis-eased, the earth and your blood literally tell the story. Deuteronomy 12:23 says that life is in the blood. This, we know, is a scientific fact. Your blood contains the source of your life. It also tells the story about its source of nutrients—the earth.

Your body was created to be a vessel for God's Spirit, not a receptacle for McDonalds. God wants your body, his temple, to remain fit and vital for his divine pleasurable purposes. God wants you to live a long and prosperous life. It pleases God immensely to see you prosper and to live a life of vitality. God uses your body and life like an advertisement for his image and likeness. What does your body and life say to others about God? Would you want your body and life on a billboard? Would God? If not, why not?

Our lives speak volumes! Everything in the universe speaks! Everything, including our individual lives, tells a unique story. What story is your life telling the world? What story are others hearing? What story are you hearing? You cannot hear your body speak so long as you are unaware of its voice! Get rid of the toxins in your body and allow your body to speak its true message.

When we began this program, we both underwent a compete body cleanse. We proposed to free our bodies of all the toxic chemicals, hormones, antibiotics, metals, etc. that we had ingested through our poor dietary habits. We are not teachers who talk the talk but refuse to walk the walk. What we teach our students, we ourselves have experienced first-hand. What we found most interesting about our cleanse process was that our bodies began to speak, and speak a lot. When we reintroduced things back into our diets; things that didn't seem to be troublesome for our digestive system before became sources of discomfort. We had no idea that our bodies were struggling to digest certain foods. We had no idea that our bodies' voices were being silenced beneath the weight of our diseased and disordered lives. Again, our bodies have voices—unfortunately, most of us are un-mindful of their presence. Most of us are refusing to hear them!

With the rise of obesity, heart disease, diabetes, and cancer, it's abundantly clear that we are neglecting to hear our body's cry for help! Hosea 4:6 tells us that people are destroyed because they lack knowledge, and more importantly; because they have rejected knowledge. It is apparent that our nation can no longer afford to turn a blind eye or a deaf ear to the voices of reason and logic. The lower brains of good men and women are hijacking their higher brain's ability to discern what is prudent from what is not.

The *First IAM*® and the *IAM*Renewed4Life® programs are designed to make people aware of their whole person—their new being—their *First IAM* self and in so doing, exchange their dying and decaying body for a new and vital *higher body and mind*! We believe the world is ripe for reaping a bountiful harvest of renewed minds, bodies, and souls! Are you one of them? Will you be one of them? We pray that you will!

The Voice of the Body

Romans 6:19 says,

> Don't you realize that your body is the temple of the Holy Spirit, who lives in you and was given to you by God? (NLT)

First Peter 2:5 says,

> And you are living stones that God is building into his spiritual temple. What's more, you are his holy priests. (NLT)

First Corinthians 3:16 says,

> Don't you realize that all of you together are the temple of God and that the Spirit of God lives in you? (NLT)

Your cells, nerves, bacteria, and various receptors of your body, all speak and communicate with one another in an effort to maintain balance in the body. When your diet and lifestyle are out of balance, your body does its dead-level best to correct the imbalance. Specific biological systems were designed by God to protect your body against disease and illness.

The cells of your body speak a very specific language. Your genes are more than simply markers that identify your unique attributes such as the color of your hair, your height, skin tone, eye color, and body definition and composition—they hold the memory of your God divine design and blueprint for your entire life.

The substances that you eat, drink, and breathe all have an effect on your cells. Just as the cells of your body speak their own language, each of these substances speaks its own language as well. Your body was designed to eat foods that are natural and whole.

Genesis 1:29-30 says,

> God said, Behold, I have given you every herb bearing seed, which is upon the face of all the earth, and every tree, in the which is the fruit of a tree yielding seed; to you it shall be for meat. And to every beast of the earth, and to every fowl of the air, and to every thing that creepeth upon the earth, wherein there is life, I have given every green herb for meat: and it was so. (KJV)

Your body speaks its native language of whole foods such as vegetables, fruits, nuts, and whole grains. Your body doesn't know the foreign language of sugar, processed foods, artificial sweeteners, and enriched flour. When you do harm to your body by over-eating, eating toxic and chemically processed foods, smoking tobacco, abusing drugs and alcohol, obsessing and worrying over things, and refusing to rest and relax, your cells don't know what to do with that information.

When you habitually keep introducing these substances to your cells, you do harm to your body's own defense systems; worse still, you mar Gods image and likeness within his temple—your body. God created your body for a divine purpose! Your body was created to thrive and feel good—not writhe from metabolic toxicity, cellular dysfunction, and poisoning!

Your body speaks to you on a regular basis; letting you know how you are doing in your daily diet, exercise routine, and lifestyle. It's important not only to hear it speak, but to begin to speak its native language by eating its natural and preferred sources of nutrition and energy.

Luke 8:18 says,

> Take heed therefore how ye hear. (KJV)

How we hear matters and when we fail to listen to the wisdom of our bodies, we find ourselves in a state of disease and disorder. Dis-ease and dis-order are not constructs of God. Your body is a marvelous machine. If you begin to speak its native language by feeding it the right foods at the right time and in the right amounts, then you will begin to witness just how resilient your body really is.

A Shack or a Temple?

How many of us would enjoy going to worship at a rundown and falling-to-pieces church or temple? What would that mean for our stewardship as parishioners? How many of us would care to live in a shack without running water or electricity? Sadly, many of our houses are better cared for than our bodies—God's temples.

At present, Leah and I own a highly successful real estate brokerage firm in North Texas. We know a little something about land and houses. We have a keen eye for a home versus a house. In our market, houses get listed daily but homes are what sell. It is possible to own a house, but it's another thing entirely to make a house a home. The same law applies to our bodies. Anyone can have a super fit and beautiful body but would the Spirit of God want to live there? That's the real question. The same rule goes for dis-eased and dis-functional bodies. We wouldn't want to live in a house without electricity and water, therefore, why would God?

Revelation 4:5-6 says,

> Out from the throne came flashes of lightning and rumblings and peals of thunder, and in front of the throne seven blazing torches burned, which are the seven Spirits of God [the sevenfold Holy Spirit]; And in front of the throne there was also what looked like a transparent glassy sea, as if of crystal. (AMP)

Does this illustration of God's temple in the book of Revelation resemble your mind, body, and soul? If not, why not? You were created to be a powerful and dynamic vessel of God's Spirit; a beautiful image and likeness of God in the flesh! God's image must be reflected in every word you speak and every action you take. It is your reasonable service and duty to a God who loves you lavishly![85]

The Voice of Energy—Mitochondria

Revelation 4:5-6 tells us that our body, God's temple, is a force of powerful energy! Your very cells tell the story of your life. In the beginning, when you were formed in the womb of your mother, you began your life journey as a single cell. Within that cell was the divine wisdom of God at work.[86]

Without getting too scientific, within every one of your body's cells exist tiny organelles known as mitochondria. As a matter of fact, mitochondria are so small you cannot see them with the naked eye. And yet, they are known as the powerhouses of the cell. Without mitochondria, we couldn't walk, talk, breathe, think, or live. We need this divine energy to survive. Mitochondria are the energy makers of our bodies. This energy is a complex chemical known as adenosine triphosphate (ATP).

There are some cells that contain hundreds to several thousand mitochondria. The number of mitochondria depends largely on what the cell needs to do. For instance, if the sole purpose of the cell is to transmit nerve impulses—as neurons do—there will be fewer mitochondria in that cell than in a muscle cell that needs tons of energy. And what's really fascinating is that, if the cell feels it's not getting enough energy to survive, more mitochondria are created.

---

85 Romans 12:1

86 Psalms 139:13-16

In addition, mitochondria act like a digestive system that takes nutrients inside, breaks them down, and then creates the (ATP) energy for the cell. This process of creating cell energy is known as *cellular respiration*.[87] Cellular respiration requires three steps: (1) glycolysis, (2) the Krebs cycle—discovered by the 1953 Nobel Prize winner, Sir Hans Adolf Krebs, and (3) electron transport chain.[88] It's the Krebs cycle which provides us with the evidence of God's wisdom within the very cell of mankind.

For instance, there are at least eight complex chemical reactions that take place during the Krebs cycle. If anything goes wrong in any one of the reactions, the whole cycle will come to a complete stop. In addition, if the reactions do not take place in the correct order, ATP will stop being produced. Hence, no energy will be produced. This system is far too complex for it to be attributed to some random act of nature. Scientists do not know how this brilliant system works—but we know. God, the intelligent designer of heaven and earth, is the wisdom, the intelligence, the architect of this highly sophisticated work of art called the Krebs cycle of cellular respiration. Genesis 2:7 says, "God breathed life into man, and man started breathing." Ecclesiastes 12:7 says that when we die, our bodies return to the dust from which it was formed, and our life-giving breath returns to its base source. God is the Energy creating the energy of our bodies!

Mitochondria help your body turn food into energy. Thus, what you feed your body and feel in your body matters greatly to your overall health! When mitochondria are functioning healthily, our body functions healthily also. When it is compromised through our unhealthy lifestyle practices, our body becomes diseased and ill.

---

87 "Cellular Respiration," *Wikipedia, the Free Encyclopedia*, http://en.wikipedia.org/w/index.php?title=Cellular_respiration&oldid=438993370 (accessed July 2010)

88 "Citric Acid," *Wikipedia, the Free Encyclopedia*, http://en.wikipedia.org/w/index.php?title=Citric_acid_cycle&oldid=433638126 (accessed July 2010)

According to Dr. David Perlmutter, mitochondria impact our moods, vitality, our aging process, longevity, and how we die. They eliminate old cells and replenish the body with new ones. They are influenced by diet, the number of calories we eat in a day, our exercise, our specific nutrients, and spiritual practice. Restored and healthy mitochondria help the cells express the genes that promote brain health and physical longevity.

Brain health is our top priority. Our brain is the seat of spiritual enlightenment and wisdom. Lifestyle factors actually modify our genetic expression by shutting off the genes that predispose us to malignancy and disease. Our mitochondria regulate the switching on and off of these genes.[89] Thus, we need highly functional mitochondria if we are going to experience our highest purpose in life. Your overall health affects the potentiality and capability of your divine design and purpose!

Listening to your body's source of energy can make a tremendous difference in the way you think, act, and respond to life's challenges and opportunities for exponential growth and prosperity! Are you listening?

The Voice of Energy—Metabolism

Metabolism is a series of processes by which food is converted into the energy and products needed to sustain life.[90] Energy is found in the calories we consume. These calories are converted into fuel that the body needs in order to maintain itself. Whether you are eating, drinking, sleeping, or working, your body is in a constant state of burning calories to keep you functioning.

Metabolism is greatly affected by your body's make up. By *make-up* we mean your body's build type; your muscle to fat ratio. Muscles require

---

89 David Perlmutter, M.D., F.A.C.N.,and Alberto Villoldo, PhD., *Power Up Your Brain: The Neuroscience of Enlightenment,* Hay House, Inc., 1st Edition 2011, United States

90 Encarta Dictionary English North America, (Version 2009)

more fuel than fat. Thus, people who strengthen their muscles daily burn more calories than those who simply diet without exercise or strength training. In addition, individuals who combine diet, cardio, and strength training exercises daily, have a faster metabolism than those who do mild to moderate cardio and diet only.[91]

We destroy our bodies' metabolism by going on and off yo-yo diets, diets that starve the body of necessary vitamins and nutrients. Listen to us; *God never intended for you to starve your body.* A five hundred calorie a day diet is not healthy for your body or your mind. And let's not forget our goal: our goal is to maintain brain health in order to fulfill the good and perfect will of God's divine design for our lives!

Your brain needs a huge assortment of nutrients, and a McDonald's value meal isn't going to provide it with those nutrients. The opposite of over-eating is starvation, and when you starve your body, you starve your brain. Eating a low-caloric meal doesn't mean you have to starve yourself to death. Again, your cells need calories for the conversion of energy. If the calories we are consuming are empty, meaning useless for energy conversion, then our cells can't provide the body with the energy it needs most to survive.

As soon as you begin the starvation process, the material body begins a cascade of metabolic events that *cry out* in an attempt to propel the body to eat. Once our lower brains are made aware of our hunger and state of starvation, they kick into overdrive, at which point we have absolutely no conscious control over the chemical reactions released throughout our bodies. The same part of your brain that controls your flight-or-flight chemical response is the same part of your brain that responds to your starvation. Once this process is triggered, the mental gymnastics and justifications begin!

---

91 www.usatoday.com/news/health/weightloss/2010-07-27-fitness-metabolism_N.htm, Article first printed in the July/August 2010 issue of Fitness magazine, *10 Tips to boost your metabolism, Maura Kelly*

How many times have we had the same conversation with the voices in our own heads regarding our weight, our finances, our marriages, our career paths? In the last chapter we clearly demonstrated that reptiles can and do speak. All we have to do to hear them is turn up our spiritual hearing aid. Your reptilian brain, when faced with starvation, speaks to your emotional brain loud and clear, and before you know it, you're over-eating to appease its irrational and emotional demands. Again, one can certainly reduce one's daily caloric intake and frankly, we all should reduce the calories we consume, most especially our sugar intake; however, there is a healthy threshold that one must take into consideration when doing so, otherwise disaster is certain. Remember, God expects us to live a life of balance. We can reduce our calories, lose weight, and enjoy our favorite foods without starving our bodies of the necessary nutrients and calories they need to thrive! Trust us, we do it every day!

According to Dharma Singh Khalsa, MD, author of the book, *Brain Longevity: The Breakthrough Medical Program that Improves Your Mind and Memory*, says that what's good for the heart is good for the head.[92] We wish to take Dr. Khalsa's mantra a little further and say to you: feed your brain what you would feed God's heart! Your body is God's and this includes your heart![93] Would you serve God two-all-beef-patties-special sauce-lettuce-cheese-pickles-onions-on-a-sesame-seed-bun? Or would you attempt to do a little better than that? You need to eat right for the image and likeness of the living God which resides within your mortal body! We propose that if you follow this rule of thumb regularly, you will not only lose weight but become healthier in the process!

Again, feed your body as if you were feeding the living God! As you do, listen carefully as your metabolism begins not only to speak, but to shout for joy! Your body wants to work efficiently, and with little

92 Dharma Singh Khalsa, MD, *Brain Longevity: The Breakthrough Medical Program that Improves your Mind and Memory,* New York, United States, May 1999

93 1 Corinthians 6:20

effort on your part, you can learn to speak its love language, which is energy.

In addition, we can avoid feeling ashamed and embarrassed by our mishaps and errors in judgment regarding our diets and lifestyle choices by simply remaining cognizant of God's image and likeness—the *First IAM* within. If we allow this voice to speak to our fearful and hungry lower minds, we will retain our dominion and authority over God's garden—our *higher minds*! Are you listening?

The Voice of Balance

The abbreviation pH stands for *power of hydrogen*. It is a measurement of acidity or alkalinity in which the pH of pure water is 7, with lower numbers indicating acidity (0 equaling maximum acidity) and higher numbers indicating alkalinity (14 equaling maximum alkalinity). A pH scale ranges from pH 0 to pH 14, with pH 7 being neutral. Values lower than 7 indicate acidity; those higher than 7 indicate alkalinity.

The body's cells each have an optimum pH level. At rest, the normal blood pH of a human being is slightly alkaline, with a pH around 7.4 on the pH scale. Anything above that value is considered alkaline; anything below is described as acidic. Acidity, to the extreme, is life-threatening for the human body. If the pH value of the body drops below 6.8 or increases above 7.8, the cells of the body cannot function properly and the human will eventually die.

The pH levels of our bodies affects every cell in our bodies. A constantly imbalanced pH level won't be tolerated by our internal system or by our entire metabolic process. Both of these systems depend heavily on a healthy alkaline environment through proper pH balance. Consuming too many unhealthy, acid forming or acidic foods, such as sugar, flour, and processed foods, can cause an overgrowth of harmful bacteria, fungi, yeasts and other micro organisms. An internal pH imbalance results in diseases such as obesity, auto-immune deficiencies, allergies, chronic fatigue and a whole host of other illnesses, diseases, and disorders of the body and brain.

Our bodies were designed to heal themselves. Thus, when our internal metabolic systems and balances are compromised, our bodies use whatever means necessary to correct imbalances due to our poor diet and lifestyle choices. For instance, we create fat cells to carry acids away from our vital organs. This, in turn, leads to obesity, which creates a whole other set of issues for the body. The absorption of undigested proteins due to an overly acidic body causes allergic reactions to foods, the environment, etc. In addition, when we have overly acidic bodies, toxins are produced and the body's ability to produce enzymes and hormones is weakened. If just one of the aforementioned issues were created within our bodies, it would be enough to severely impact our daily lives. Unfortunately for some individuals, all three of these imbalances are present and wreak havoc on their bodies' day in and day out. A diet which consists of a proper acid-alkaline balance of foods will help transform your body's pH balance from dangerously acidic to healthily (slightly) alkaline. In addition, you should add plenty of alkaline water to your daily diet.

According to *Balance-pH-Diet.com,*[94] a proper alkaline diet suggests taking in at least 80 percent of alkaline foods, like green vegetables or grasses, and never more than 20 percent of neutral and acidic foods. Eating green foods, vegetables and alkaline foods will help our internal fluids achieve a natural pH balance, as the acidic environment inside the body will be eliminated. That means, by eating vegetables all day long, or taking sprouted greens dietary supplements and avoiding acid forming and acidic foods, the body's pH level will gradually be balanced. When pH balance is achieved, your body will start to restore its overall health.[95]

Our body's pH level speaks to us, but are we listening? If you have chronic pain, arthritis, osteoporosis, chronic fatigue, low energy, heart

---

94 http://balance-ph-diet.com/May 2011

95 Genesis 1:29-30

arrhythmia issues, allergies, acne, frequent illnesses like colds, infections, bronchitis, headaches, or if you're overweight, you might want to listen to the voice of your body's natural balance system. It's trying to tell you that you are out of balance internally. Are you listening?

With very little effort, you can re-balance and replenish your body's natural chemistry. Your tiny effort can mean the difference between a lifetime of pain and suffering versus a lifetime of vitality and success!

The Voice of Elimination

Our lives have become toxic. How they have become toxic is a matter of serious contemplation; suffice it to say, however, that we are indeed toxic. We need elimination! Without proper elimination of these toxic memories, ideas, beliefs, and attitudes, we become depressed, oppressed, and diseased in our minds and our bodies. God has given us several ingenious ways to process and disseminate healthy matter while eliminating and releasing toxic and harmful substances.

For instance, crying is a wonderful way to release tension, fear, sadness, and grief. Expressing our anger is a helpful tool to eliminate rage, bitterness, and resentment—emotions that can become strongholds in our lives; strongholds which lead to depression and or physical ailments of the body. Laughter is a wonderful mechanism that helps alleviate stress. Laughter causes us to use a multitude of muscles in the body and causes our brains to release its natural tranquilizers, pain relievers, and endorphins—the body's innate "happy chemicals." These are all ways in which the voice of elimination makes itself known to us. Are we listening?

In addition, our bodies' own digestive and urinary systems play critical roles in our bodies' overall health and vitality. We must be able to eliminate the toxic substances that we bombard our bodies with daily—from our environment, our processed foods, our alcohol consumption. Again, we need elimination—more importantly, we need effective elimination!

Your gut is a common culprit in the development of disease and illness. A balanced digestive system will balance your body. A healthy gut strengthens your immunity via a healthy and proper pH balance. It maintains the integrity of your intestinal tract lining. It enhances your body's own detoxification system and it helps manufacture essential vitamins and nutrients like vitamins B and K.

Yeast and fungus in the body (due to poor diet and pH imbalance) cause a weakened immune system. Our immune system is our body's defense system against disease and various disorders. Yeast and fungal overgrowths are the result of Candida, which kills our "friendly bacteria." We need good bacteria in our intestines and when we take antibiotics due to our failed immune system, we kill the good bugs along with the bad.

When we eat processed beef and poultry, or drink city water, these sources are all full of toxic chemicals, antibiotics, pesticides, and steroidal hormones. These toxic substances strip our gut of the "good guy" bacteria leaving us vulnerable and susceptible to all sorts of disease and illness.

Malabsorption syndrome is an insufficient production of digestive enzymes by the pancreas, or by the small intestine. A decreased production of bile, too much acid in the stomach, or too many of the wrong kinds of bacteria growing in the small intestine may also interfere with digestion. Undigested meat causes damage to your stomach lining. Starches, if they are not properly digested, ferment in the stomach and feed the negative bacteria which causes boating.[96] Eventually, malabsorption leads to inflammation in the gut.

More than one hundred million Americans take proton pump inhibitors (PPIs) to deal with acid reflux, ulcers, and heartburn. PPIs work by reducing the amount of stomach acid your body produces. However, PPIs interfere with your body's natural absorption of

---

96 http://www.merckmanuals.com/home/sec09/ch125/ch125a.html

protein and vital nutrients, more importantly, magnesium. As a matter of fact, the Food and Drug Administration issued a warning that taking a PPI for a prolonged period may cause severe magnesium deficiencies.[97]

Magnesium is an essential element for your body's overall health. It relaxes your blood vessels, thereby regulating your blood pressure. Symptoms of magnesium deficiency include: hyper excitability, muscle weakness and fatigue. Severe magnesium deficiency can cause hypocalcaemia, low serum potassium levels (hypokalemia), retention of sodium, low circulating levels of PTH, neurological and muscular symptoms (tremor, muscle spasms, tetany), loss of appetite, nausea, vomiting, personality changes and death from heart failure. Magnesium plays an important role in carbohydrate metabolism and its deficiency may worsen insulin resistance, a condition that often precedes diabetes, or may be a consequence of insulin resistance.[98]

Many of the aforementioned issues are due in part to an enzyme deficiency suffered by many Americans. Every function of our body is enzyme dependent. The pancreas and enzymes work together to break down our foods in order to get the nutrients our body needs to our cells, tissues, and organs.

There are three main reasons for poor enzymatic release in the body: diet, age, and energy. Any food that is cooked, processed, or micro-waved above 118°F, loses all of the benefits of its natural enzymes. We are born with a set number of enzymes, and when they're gone—they're gone for good. In addition, as we grow older, our bodies produce fewer enzymes. Luckily for our bodies, God created certain foods full of enzymes that replenish our bodies' daily enzymatic expenditures. However, because

97 www.fda.gov/Safety/MedWatch/SafetyInformation/SafetyAlertsforHumanMedicalProducts

98 "Magnesium Deficiency," *Wikipedia, the Free Encyclopedia,* http://en.wikipedia.org/wiki/Magnesium_deficiency_(medicine) "(accessed June 2010)

of our poor diet choices and the way in which we cook and prepare our foods, our foods offer us little enzymatic support. Research on aging is demonstrating that the aging process can be altered by simply replenishing one's enzyme balance by taking supplemental enzymes with every meal.[99] A significant amount of the body's energy is expended during the digestive process. When you eat, your digestive system breaks down food into energy to fuel your body according to its needs for functionality and repair. Without the proper function of enzymes, your food isn't able to be fully digested, which leads to bloating, gas, and indigestion. A lack of enzymes allows your body's balance to become compromised; leading to the production of dangerous by-products in the body which can lead to food allergies, yeast overgrowth, and harmful bacteria which cause disease and dysfunction in the body.

The voices of enzyme deficiency are: acid reflux disease, bloating, constipation, irritable bowel syndrome, cramping, diarrhea, food allergies, gas, heartburn, nausea, water retention, and weight gain. By listening to our bodies speak, we can alter the aging process and eliminate disease and discomfort from our lives—in some cases, immediately!

The Law of Dieting versus the Grace of Healthy Living

God isn't looking for perfect figures and muscular hard bodies any more than God is asking us to build and erect elaborate temples throughout our cities. God is seeking a people with humble and contrite hearts, people who are willing to be used of God for his divine purpose.[100] God is seeking a people who love beyond measure and demonstrate compassion for those that are without hope and are in the greatest need.

---

99 http://www.nia.nih.gov/healthinformation/publications/preventaging.htm, *Health Publication, Can We Prevent Aging July 2010*

100 Isaiah 66:2

Acts 4:32 says,

> The whole congregation of believers was united as one—one heart, one mind! They didn't even claim ownership of their own possessions. No one said, "That's mine; you can't have it." They shared everything. (MSG)

For now, this world's economy is run by men who are oblivious to their *First I AM higher self image;* however, there will come a day when this earth will become *one* in spirit and truth.[101] Until then, those of us who are keenly aware of our true self have a job to do—live our *God lives* out loud and proud![102] One of the best ways to accomplish this task is to live healthy and fruitful lives so others take note! Notice we didn't say diet or count calories—we said live healthily and fruitfully.

There is a huge difference between dieting and healthy living. Dieting is a man-made law or construct—it's restrictive by its very nature and doesn't allow for liberty of mind, body, and spirit. When we diet, we begin in a state of fear and deprivation; a feeling which cannot succeed. Healthy living and a truly nutritional lifestyle, on the other hand, are liberating and fall in line with God's divine design for our lives.

Genesis 1:28 says,

> Prosper! Reproduce! Fill the Earth! Take charge! Be responsible for fish in the sea and birds in the air, for every living thing that moves on the face of Earth. (MSG)

God wants us to live a life of abundance not a life of lack or deprivation. Dieting is not of God—period! Dieting, just like the Mosaic law of the Old Testament, fails to liberate and free. Only a life filled with Spirit can accomplish true liberty and freedom from our old unhealthy strongholds; whether they be food, alcohol, or otherwise.

---

[101] Revelation 21:1

[102] Matthew 5:14-16

Dieting *inflames* the lower reptilian and mammalian brains, whereas healthy living *changes* all three brains physiologically, psychologically, and spiritually. Dieting forces us to focus on the self—the lower self. Certainly God wants us to focus our attention on living a life of health and fitness—doing so requires dedication and commitment, however, the number on our bathroom scale or the size of our waistband shouldn't supersede God's law of abundance and prosperity.

God's Perfect Design for the Body

Genesis 2:7 says,

> The LORD God formed man of the dust of the ground, and breathed into his nostrils the breath of life; and man became a living soul. (KJV)

This verse has actually two parts just as we demonstrated earlier with Genesis 1:27. Let us explain.

1) The LORD God formed man of the dust of the ground,
2) And breathed into his nostrils the breath of life; and man became a living soul.

Thus, according to this text, man has a body and a spirit. Our body evolved from the earth—from its base elements. God's breath is Spirit.[103] God's Spirit is our life source!

Second Corinthians 5:1-9 says,

> For we know that when this earthly tent we live in is taken down (that is, when we die and leave this earthly body), we will have a house in heaven, an eternal body made for us by God himself and not by human hands. We grow weary in our present bodies, and we long to put on our heavenly bodies like new clothing. For we will put on

[103] Job 32:8

> heavenly bodies; we will not be spirits without bodies. While we live in these earthly bodies, we groan and sigh, but it's not that we want to die and get rid of these bodies that clothe us. Rather, we want to put on our new bodies so that these dying bodies will be swallowed up by life. God himself has prepared us for this, and as a guarantee he has given us his Holy Spirit. So we are always confident, even though we know that as long as we live in these bodies we are not at home with the Lord. For we live by believing and not by seeing. Yes, we are fully confident, and we would rather be away from these earthly bodies, for then we will be at home with the Lord. So whether we are here in this body or away from this body, our goal is to please him. (NLT)

Our bodies were created for the Spirit of God to dwell. Your spirit, God's image and likeness in you, is the real you. Your earthly body is *not* the real you! Yes, your body is incredible. Yes, God designed your body to perform incredible functions, day in and day out. And even as incredible as your body is, your body is simply a tent or covering for the real you—the *First I AM you!*

As 2 Corinthians 5:9 states, our highest goal in life is to please the one who gives us our being-ness. Without God, our bodies are completely useless; a fact made self evident by today's increased numbers of child on-set obesity and chronic diseases and disorders. Our young people are sick and getting sicker with each passing day! Sugar, flour, refined, processed, and fast foods are destroying our children's future. Tragically, we adults are aiding and abetting in the slow destruction of these tiny temples of God by allowing them to eat poorly and live unhealthily without deliberation and intention. Could there be any greater sin than slowly poisoning our children? Unfortunately, that's exactly what we are doing when we allow them to drink and eat sugar without moderation, or more importantly, self restraint and control.

Romans 6:13 says

> Do not let any part of your body become an instrument of evil to serve sin. Instead, give yourselves completely to God, for you

> were dead, but now you have new life. So use your whole body as an instrument to do what is right for the glory of God. (NLT)

Because children find it nearly impossible to police themselves, we, their adult spiritual sponsors, must be their garrisons. Taking our children to children's church Sunday morning isn't enough! Not only do they need a true understanding of their *higher self image* in God, they need to understand what it means to abide in that image, day in and day out—this includes their diet! Children will follow our lead—good, bad, or indifferent. We can assure those who are parents or overseers of children, you will be held accountable for how you cared for these little temples of God.[104]

Romans 12:1 says,

> Give your bodies to God because of all he has done for you. Let them be a living and holy sacrifice—the kind he will find acceptable. This is truly the way to worship him. (NLT)

Elizabeth Gilbert, in her acclaimed book, *Eat, Pray, Love,*[105] said, "I want God to play in my bloodstream the way sunlight amuses itself on the water." Our body is God's home. Our body is God's temple. Our body is God's vessel and tool. If God isn't playing in your bloodstream like sunlight amuses itself on water, you're not living—you're merely existing and poorly existing at that!

If you will allow God to infiltrate your entire being—inside and out, no matter the cost—you will be made whole: *complete, including all parts or aspects, with nothing left out; not divided into parts and not regarded as consisting of separate parts*! Your *First IAM body* is waiting for you. Can you hear it call out to you? All that's left to do is simply answer and receive it!

---

104 Mark 9:42

105 Elizabeth Gilbert *Eat, Pray, Love*, (Penguin Group, 2006), New York, United States

Chapter 5

THE *FIRST IAM* HIGHER SELF LIFE

In the last chapter, we introduced the *First IAM higher self body*. We learned that our bodies have an intelligent voice and operating system that, when fully understood and acknowledged, has the ability to lead us into complete and total health and wholeness. More significantly, we learned that God's *highest image* and *likeness* abides within our physical bodies and that great care must be given to our bodies to ensure that God's perfect and acceptable will is made manifest to a darkened world. In the next chapter, we will discover what the *First IAM higher self life* looks like.

The *First* Day

The Genesis creation narrative is our blueprint for the *higher life* in the *First IAM* identity. Let's review that life together shall we?

Genesis 1:1-5 says,

> In the beginning God created the heaven and the earth. And the earth was without form, and void; and darkness was upon the face of the deep. And the Spirit of God moved upon the face of the waters. And God said, Let there be light: and there was light. And God saw the light, that it was good: and God divided the light from the darkness. And God called the light Day, and the darkness he called Night. And the evening and the morning were the first day. (KJV)

Thirteen times the word *light* is employed in this one chapter alone, thirty-five times in the book of Job, and three hundred and nine times throughout the Bible. We believe the redundant use of the word *light* is a vital key to a deep mystery concerning the true identity of mankind. We believe God's *I AM* identity is this light energy; the very wisdom which *enlightens* the very minds and hearts of men regarding their *highest self and life*!

John 1:6-14 says,

> There was a man sent from God, whose name was John. The same came for a witness, to bear witness of the Light, that all men through *him* might believe. He [John] was not that Light, but was sent to bear witness of that Light [Him]. That was the true Light, which lighteth every man that cometh into the world. *He* was in the world, and the world was made by *him*, and the world knew *him* not. *He* came unto *his* own, and *his* own received *him* not. But as many as received *him*, to *them* gave he power to become the sons of God, even to *them* that believe on *his name*: Which were born, not of blood, nor of the will of the flesh, nor of the will of man, but of God. And the Word was made flesh, and *dwelt among us*, (and we beheld his glory, the glory as of *the only begotten* of the Father,) full of grace and truth. (KJV)

Here, we see the words, *him* and *them* together again. If you recall from Chapter 2, *The First IAM Higher Self Image,* we discussed these two very distinct identifiers of Genesis 1:27a and 1:27b. We stated that the words *he him* of the first segment (designated as Genesis 1:27a) represented the *higher self image* of God in mankind whereas the words *he them* of segment two (designated as Genesis 1:27b) represented the lower material self image of mankind.

First John 1:5 says,

> God is Light. (KJV)

Matthew 5:14-16 says,

> *Ye are the light* of the world. A city that is set on a hill cannot be hid. Neither do men light a candle, and put it under a bushel, but on a candlestick; and it giveth light unto all that are in the house. Let your light so shine before men, that they may see your good works, and glorify your Father which is in heaven. (KJV)

John 8:12 says,

> *I am the light* of the world: he that followeth me shall not walk in darkness, but shall have the light of life. (KJV)

Ephesians 5:8-18 says,

> For ye were sometimes darkness, but now <u>are ye light in the Lord</u>: walk as children of light: (For the fruit of the Spirit is in all goodness and righteousness and truth;) Proving what is acceptable unto the Lord. And have no fellowship with the unfruitful works of darkness, but rather reprove them. For it is a shame even to speak of those things which are done of them in secret. But all things that are reproved are made manifest by the light: for whatsoever doth make manifest is light. Wherefore he saith, Awake thou that sleepest, and arise from the dead, and *Christ shall give thee light.* See then that ye walk circumspectly, not as fools, but as wise, Redeeming the time, because the days are evil. Wherefore be ye not unwise, but understanding what the will of the Lord is. And be not drunk with wine, wherein is excess; but be filled with the Spirit. (KJV)

We have this *light* within us! Per the Bible, God is Light. The *light* is our *highest self image* and *likeness.* And like John the Baptist, we were created to *bear witness of this light* (he him), God's glory.

On the first day of creation, before God does anything—creates anything—He evokes *light* to enter our material universe! God's very essence and presence scatters darkness and eliminates chaos and emptiness. God speaks and bondage, poverty, illness, and disorder disappear in a nanosecond. The word of wisdom was made to indwell flesh and blood. Living a life void of our *First IAM higher self image* is like living in a house where electricity is available but choosing to never flip a switch. Why do we choose to walk around in darkness? Doesn't that seem a bit crazy?

Matthew 6:22 says,

> The light of the body is the eye: if therefore thine eye be single, thy whole body shall be full of light. (KJV)

Interestingly enough, the retina is a light-sensitive tissue lining the inner surface of the eye. The optics of the eye create an image of the visual world on the retina, which serves much the same function as film in a camera. Light striking the retina initiates a cascade of chemical and electrical events that ultimately trigger nerve impulses. These are sent to various visual centers of the brain through the fibers of the optic nerve. Several important features of visual perception can be traced to the retinal encoding and processing of light.[106] In addition, the retina contains approximately one hundred million neurons. A neuron is an electrically excitable cell that processes and transmits information by electrical and chemical signaling. Neurons connect to each other to form networks. Neurons are the core components of the nervous system, which includes the brain, spinal cord, and peripheral ganglia.[107]

Understanding how the eye processes light to create perception is extremely fascinating. Jesus was right; how we see does in fact affect how we perceive our world, and more importantly, how we perceive and receive God's essence, which is *the light of all men*. What we need is God's eye. We need God's vision for our *higher life!*

---

106 "Retina," *Wikipedia, the Free Encyclopedia* http://en.wikipedia.org/wiki/Retina, (accessed May 2011)

107 "Retina," *Wikipedia, the Free Encyclopedia*, http://en.wikipedia.org/wiki/Retina, (accessed May 2011)

In order for us to experience God's vision for our *higher life* design, we have to see what God sees. God's eye is one of unity—not duality. As we have discovered, the common theme of Scripture is oneness or at-one-ment in Spirit. The Tree of the Knowledge of Good and Evil, on the other hand, causes division—double vision for those whose eyes are not single toward God. In fact, the Tree of the Knowledge of Good and Evil causes blindness—spiritual *higher self* and *life* blindness, without the oversight of God's wisdom and unified vision. The Tree of the Knowledge of Good and Evil, under the wrong economy, produces a false and deadly value system. A false and deadly value system calls things which are good evil and things which are evil—good. It also substitutes darkness for light and light for darkness.[108] There is a very subtle difference between God's law and man's interpretation of God's law.

Genesis 3:1-3 says,

> Now the serpent was more subtil than any beast of the field which the LORD God had made. And he said unto the woman, Yea, hath God said, Ye shall not eat of every tree of the garden? And the woman said unto the serpent, We may eat of the fruit of the trees of the garden: But of the fruit of the tree which is in the midst of the garden, God hath said, Ye shall not eat of it, neither shall ye touch it, lest ye die. (KJV)

Genesis 2:16-17 says,

> Of every tree of the garden thou mayest freely eat: But of the tree of the knowledge of good and evil, thou shalt not eat of it: for in the day that thou eatest thereof thou shalt surely die. (KJV)

God never said Adam couldn't touch the tree. God simply *warned* them of the consequences of eating its fruit. The fruit of the Tree of

---

108 Isaiah 5:20

the Knowledge of Good and Evil was deadly—but why? Surely God wants us to evaluate good and evil—right? Yes![109] And doesn't God want us to choose good and hate evil? Yes![110] Then what gives—why was the fruit deadly?

The Tree of the Knowledge of Good and Evil provided one with knowledge of good and evil—that's a fact. Knowledge, however, whether good or evil—without spiritual wisdom, understanding, and discernment—is a recipe for disaster. Interpreting God's word (Scripture) without the employment of one's *higher mind* is complete and utter foolishness.[111]

Paul, in 1 Corinthians 6:12, said this regarding the consequences of subordinating our *higher self image*

> You say, "I am allowed to do anything"—but not everything is good for you. And even though "I am allowed to do anything," I must not become a slave to anything. (NLT)

Adam made the decision to subordinate God's glorious image within himself to the voices of his lower minds (reptile/Eve). As a result, Adam judged God's word (truth) by the flawed value system of his lower material environment rather than by the ever present help of his *higher self and mind,* and the result was spiritual estrangement.[112] How tragic for Adam—how tragic for those of us who continue to follow Adam's example! It doesn't have to be this way. This can be the *first day* for our *First IAM* realization and reception. God's light can disperse the darkness of our old mind and illumine our true *higher self image* in order to manifest our *higher self life!* We don't have to go another day—not one single day—without knowing *who* and *what* we really are!

---

109 Hebrews 5:14

110 Romans 12:9

111 Romans 1:22

112 Psalm 46:1

Jeremiah 1:10 says,

> See, *today* I appoint you over nations and kingdoms to uproot and tear down, to destroy and overthrow, to build and to plant. (KJV)

Today, this first day, before another minute passes you by, you can stop the never-ending false accusations and judgments of your old world and life by simply taking dominion and authority. You have that kind of power! Use it and see what happens next!

The Separation of the *Higher* from the Lower

Several times throughout the Genesis creation narrative, God separates. God separated the light from darkness.[113] He separated the waters of the earth below from the waters of the heavens above.[114] He separated the earth from the seas.[115] He separated the day from night.[116] He separated the sun from the moon.[117] And last but certainly not least, God separated mankind from the other species of the earth.[118]

Whenever God divides, he does so in order to bring about unity. You may be asking, how can that be? How can unity come from disunity? The answer is found in the one who holds the two so as to create the One.

John 12:24-26 says,

> Verily, verily, I say unto you, Except a corn of wheat fall into the ground and *die*, it abideth *alone*: but if it die, it bringeth forth much fruit. He that loveth his life shall lose it; and he that hateth his life

113 Genesis 1:1-5
114 Genesis 1:6-8
115 Genesis 1:9-10
116 Genesis 1:14
117 Genesis 1:16-18
118 Genesis 1:26-28

> in this world shall keep it unto life eternal. If any man serve me, let him follow me; and *where I am*, there shall also my servant be: if any man serve me, him will my Father honour. (KJV)

There are two very important words (keys) we are given in this passage of Scripture; keys that illumine our way toward the *First IAM life*. The first word is the word *die*. The second word is the word *alone*.

The word *die* is the Greek word, *apothnesko*. *Apothnesko* is a derivative of two words: 1. *apo* meaning, *of separation of a part from the whole, of any kind of separation of one thing from another by which the union or fellowship of the two is destroyed*, and 2. *thnesko*, meaning *to die or be dead*.[119]

The word *alone* is the Greek word, *monos*, meaning *to be alone (without a companion), forsaken, destitute of help*.[120]

Genesis 3:9-10 says,

> God called unto Adam, and said unto him, Where art thou? And he said, I heard thy voice in the garden, and I was afraid, because I was naked; and I hid myself. (KJV)

There are two different definitions for the word *naked* in the Genesis creation narrative: (1) Genesis 2:25, and (2) Genesis 3:7. The word *naked* employed in Genesis 2:25 is the Hebrew word, *'arowm*, meaning *to be nude, without clothing*. The second use of the word *naked* in Genesis 3:7 is the Hebrew word, *eyrom*, meaning *nakedness and necessity, utterly naked and helpless*.

Recall, if you will, that the word *subtil* in the Hebrew is the word *'aruwm*. We discovered that it meant *to be cautious, prudent, and perceptive*. The serpent was *'aruwm*. The Hebrew word for naked *'arowm* has a very similar spelling to the word subtil *'aruwm*. Why do you suppose that is? What is the significance of these two very similar words?

---

119 "Apothnesko" Strong's Exhaustive Lexicon #599, 575, 2348

120 "Monos" Strong's Exhaustive Lexicon #3441

Adam was supposed to take control of his sphere of influence.[121] Adam wasn't in control—Eve was in control; more specifically, the serpent was in control of both Adam and Eve. Again, the thing that was created to *help* us can kill us if we're not *'aruwm (cautious, prudent, and perceptive)*. Adam's *helpmeet* was not very *helpful*, to say the least. As a result, Adam found himself *eyrom*—helpless and all alone, and *monos*—alone and without a companion.

In Matthew's gospel, we find that the Christ was faced with the same temptation as Adam and Eve, however, Jesus passed with flying colors.

Matthew 4:1-11 says,

> Then was Jesus led up of the Spirit into the wilderness to be tempted of the devil. And when he had fasted forty days and forty nights, he was afterward an hungred. And *when the tempter came to him*, he said, *If thou be the Son of God*, command that these stones be made bread. But he answered and said, *It is written*, Man shall not live by bread alone, but by every word that proceedeth out of the mouth of God. Then the devil taketh him up into the holy city, and setteth him on a pinnacle of the temple, And saith unto him, *If thou be the Son of God*, cast thyself down: for it is written, He shall give his angels charge concerning thee: and in their hands they shall bear thee up, lest at any time thou dash thy foot against a stone. Jesus said unto him, *It is written again*, Thou shalt not tempt the Lord thy God. Again, the devil taketh him up into an exceeding high mountain, and sheweth him all the kingdoms of the world, and the glory of them; And saith unto him, All these things will I give thee, if thou wilt fall down and worship me. Then saith Jesus unto him, *Get thee hence, Satan: for it is written*, Thou shalt worship the Lord thy God, and him only shalt thou serve. Then the devil leaveth him, and, behold, angels came and ministered unto him. (KJV)

---

121 Genesis 1:28

Each and every time the tempter came at Jesus with an accusation regarding his *First IAM* identity, Jesus answered the tempter's false charge with God's truth. Jesus didn't waste time trying to defend his nature—his *higher self image*—he knew already *who* and *what* he was and to *whom* he belonged. Jesus knew how to overcome his lower reptilian and paleomammalian brains with success. Jesus knew his God! And because Jesus knew his God—he knew his *higher self* and *life* purpose and design! In addition, knowing God as intimately as he did, he was able to employ God's most powerful weapon—his word! There is no greater power or energy in the universe than God's word, and when it's in the mouth of a *First-IAMer*—one who truly knows *who* and *what* they are—it's unstoppable![122]

Just as God spoke a division between the waters beneath from the waters above, we, too, have that same kind of power and authority to regulate our lower minds in order to maintain our *higher mind's* dominion and logic. Interestingly enough, Jesus was led into the wilderness to be tested right after his baptism. During the ritual of baptism, our material bodies are *lowered* into a body of water. This body of water is a type of grave or tomb. In addition, baptism symbolizes a cleansing or washing away of our old natures for our new and *higher natures* in God. We do this ritual to symbolize the death of our former material and lower natures; to follow after the example of Christ's death and resurrection. As we are raised *up* out of the water, we are declared raised into a new resurrected life—just as Christ was raised into his resurrected life in Spirit. While this ritual is beautiful to witness, without the right heart and mind employed, its benefits fall powerless. True salvation and resurrection come as a sum of our faith. Our faith is a matter of mind—a *higher mind* centered on the deep things of God![123]

God divides the partition of division between our *higher self image* (heavenly image) from that of our lower self image (earthly image).

---

[122] Isaiah 55:11

[123] Isaiah 26:3

Ephesians 2:14-18 says,

> For Christ (*higher self image OF GOD*) is our peace, who hath made *both one*, and hath broken down the middle wall of partition between us; Having abolished in *his* flesh the enmity, even the law of commandments contained in ordinances; for to make in *him*self of twain *one new man*, so making peace; And that he might reconcile both unto God in *one body* by the cross, having slain the enmity thereby: And came and preached peace to you which were afar off, and to *them* that were nigh. For through *him* we both have access by *one Spirit* unto the Father. (KJV)

God's acts of separation are just as common as his acts of at-one-ment. God wills that all things in heaven and earth are of one spirit—his Spirit.[124] However, we must separate ourselves from our old way of life. More times than not, God creates the chasm of separation for us. Seldom do we choose the *higher life* or the *higher self image* all by ourselves. Like the ancient Israelites, we prefer the *three hots and a cot* back in Egypt over the liberating and exhilarating life God has prepared for us!

The *Higher Life* Promised

Exodus 3:7-10 says,

> And the LORD said, I have surely seen the affliction of my people which are in Egypt, and have heard their cry by reason of their taskmasters; for I know their sorrows; And I am come down to deliver them out of the hand of the Egyptians, and to bring them up out of that land unto a good land and a large, unto a land flowing with milk and honey; unto the place of the Canaanites, and the Hittites, and the Amorites, and the Perizzites, and the Hivites, and the Jebusites. Now therefore, behold, the cry of the children of Israel is come unto me: and I have also seen

124 Ephesians 4:1-6; 5:21

the oppression wherewith the Egyptians oppress them. Come now therefore, and I will send thee unto Pharaoh, that thou mayest bring forth my people the children of Israel out of Egypt. (KJV)

Leviticus 20:24-26 says,

> Ye shall inherit their [the nations of Canaan] land, and I will give it unto you to possess it, a land that floweth with milk and honey: *I am the LORD your God, which have separated you from other people.* Ye shall therefore put difference between clean beasts and unclean, and between unclean fowls and clean: and ye shall not make your souls abominable by beast, or by fowl, or by any manner of living thing that creepeth on the ground, which I have separated from you as unclean. And ye shall be holy unto me: for I the LORD am holy, and *have severed you from other people, that ye should be mine.* (KJV)

Deuteronomy 6:1-15 says,

> Now these are the commandments, the statutes, and the judgments, which the LORD your God commanded to teach you, that ye might do them in the land whither ye go to possess it: That thou mightest fear the LORD thy God, to keep all his statutes and his commandments, which I command thee, thou, and thy son, and thy son's son, all the days of thy life; and that *thy days may be prolonged.*
>
> Hear therefore, O Israel, and observe to do it; that it may be well with thee, and that *ye may increase mightily*, as the LORD God of thy fathers hath promised thee, in *the land that floweth with milk and honey.*
>
> Hear, O Israel: *The LORD our God is one LORD*: And thou shalt love the LORD thy God with all thine heart, and with all thy soul, and with all thy might. And these words, which I command thee this day, shall be in thine heart: And *thou shalt teach them diligently*

> *unto thy children, and shalt talk of them when thou sittest in thine house, and when thou walkest by the way, and when thou liest down, and when thou risest up. And thou shalt bind them for a sign upon thine hand, and they shall be as frontlets between thine eyes. And thou shalt write them upon the posts of thy house, and on thy gates.*
>
> And it shall be, when the LORD thy God shall have brought thee into the land which he sware unto thy fathers, to Abraham, to Isaac, and to Jacob, *to give thee great and goodly cities, which thou buildedst not, And houses full of all good things, which thou filledst not, and wells digged, which thou diggedst not, vineyards and olive trees, which thou plantedst not*; when *thou shalt have eaten and be full*; Then beware lest thou forget the LORD, which brought thee forth out of the land of Egypt, from the house of bondage. Thou shalt fear the LORD thy God, and serve him, and shalt swear by his name. Ye shall not go after other gods, of *the gods of the people which are round about you* (For the LORD thy God is a jealous God *among you*). (KJV)

Deuteronomy 11:8-15 says,

> Therefore shall ye keep all the commandments which I command you this day, that ye may be strong, and go in and possess the land, whither ye go to possess it; And that ye may *prolong your days in the land*, which the LORD sware unto your fathers to give unto them <u>and to their seed</u>, a land that floweth with milk and honey. For the land, whither thou goest in to possess it, *is not as the land of Egypt*, from whence ye came out, where thou sowedst thy seed, and wateredst it with thy foot, as a garden of herbs: But the land, whither ye go to possess it, is a *land of hills and valleys, and drinketh water of the rain of heaven: A land which the LORD thy God careth for: the eyes of the LORD thy God are always upon it, from the beginning of the year even unto the end of the year.* And it shall come to pass, if ye shall hearken diligently unto my commandments which I command you this day, to love the LORD your God, and to serve him with all your heart and with all your soul, That *I will give you the rain of your land in his due season, the first rain and the latter rain, that thou mayest*

> *gather in thy corn, and thy wine, and thine oil. And I will send grass in thy fields for thy cattle, that thou mayest eat and be full.* (KJV)

How can anyone read those words and not shout hallelujah? The *higher life* of the *First IAM* is a life of abundance and exponential growth! Everything is completely provided for—there is nothing, and we mean nothing, kept back from those that love the *I AM* with their whole hearts, minds, and souls!

The *First IAM higher life* is a life worth receiving. Why on earth would we refuse to accept our *First IAM higher self image* and *life* and in the process forfeit experiencing our *highest good?*

Just in case you missed all of the blessings that God has promised us—waiting for us to experience while living and operating within our divine *First IAM self image, body, mind, and life*, we have compiled the following list: *(*Note, this list is not a complete list—it's just a list of the benefits from the aforementioned Scriptures.)*

A long and healthy life for us and our posterity

A life of exponential growth and increase

A life of power, favor, and prestige

A life of authority and dominion over our present and future potentiality

A life of prosperity without labor or toil

A full, pleasant, and peaceful life without worry

A life of protection and security without fear

A life of total provision without anxiety

Who wouldn't want the *First IAM higher life*?

Just think: of all of the things that God separated, he separated us for himself. We are his special creation. We, unlike the other living organisms of the earth, were designed to reflect God's glorious image and likeness.

Genesis 1:21-27 says,

> And God created great whales, and every living creature that moveth, which the waters brought forth abundantly, *after their kind*, and every winged fowl *after his kind*: and God saw that it was good.
>
> And God said, Let the earth bring forth the living creature *after his kind*, cattle, and creeping thing, and beast of the earth after his kind: and it was so. And God made the beast of the earth after his kind, and cattle *after their kind*, and everything that creepeth upon the earth after his kind: and God saw that it was good.
>
> And God said, Let us make man in our image, *after our likeness*: and let them have dominion over the fish of the sea, and over the fowl of the air, and over the cattle, and over all the earth, and over every creeping thing that creepeth upon the earth. So God created man in his own image, in the image of God created he him; male and female created he them. (KJV)

Do you see the words *after their kind*? Guess what? Our *kind* is God's *kind*. You were created after God's kind—His Spirit! You, the real you—the true you, the *higher you* wasn't created after *another kind*. Though our material bodies evolved after *another kind*, our true nature—our spiritual nature—evolved after the Spirit of God. Our true nature is a result of God's effectual work within our spirit-self—our *higher self* and *mind!*

Now, do you understand the gravity of Adam's error? Adam's helpmeet wasn't flesh of his flesh and bone of his bone; Adam's flesh and bone were of another *kind*. Adam's flesh was the product of the earth—the process of material evolution. Adam's true helpmeet was God's image and likeness—the only *kind*—a *kind* not of this earth. Adam's helpmeet was God's power-imbuing, provision-supplying, authority-granting, and prosperity-creating—Spirit! Adam subordinated God's image and likeness to a creature—a creature of another *kind*.[125] Adam relied upon his own substandard flesh (Eve/Serpent) for a rendering of God's truth and word. That error cost Adam his *higher life and highest self image.*

When we subordinate our *First IAM higher self image* to that of another *kind; a kind* far less superior than the glorious essence of God, we are subordinating not only our *highest self* but God's. We were made separate from our material body, our material lineage, our material world, and made perfect in God's image and likeness for his divine design.[126]

It's time for us to get serious about our true nature—our *higher nature* and reverse the Adamic curse upon our lives! It's time for us to let go of our material bodies—bodies that belong to another *kind*, a lower heredity—and press forward and upward toward our *highest kind*—our *spiritual inheritance!* But you have to receive it! You have to want it! Are you willing to fight for it?

In Genesis chapter 32, Jacob wrestles with God for his *First IAM* blessing.

Genesis 32:26-30 says:

> I will not let thee go, except thou bless me. And he [angel of the Lord] said unto him, What is thy name? And he said, Jacob. And he said, Thy name shall be called no more Jacob, but Israel: for as a prince hast thou power with God and with men, and hast prevailed. And Jacob asked him, and said, Tell me, I pray thee, thy name. And he said, Wherefore is it that thou dost ask after my name? And he blessed him there. And Jacob called the name

125 Romans 1:23

126 Romans 8:28-30

> of the place Peniel: for I have seen God face to face, and my life is preserved. (KJV)

Jacob saw God face to face and lived to tell about it. What about you? Have you seen God's face lately? Better yet, are you living to tell about it?

Your material genetics are temporary but your spiritual genetics are eternal! There's no logical reason to hold fast to that which will not and cannot last.

Let go of your past, and reach out toward heaven. Like Jacob, demand your inheritance today and live a *higher life* which speaks volumes to God's goodness and love!

Go look into your mirror! Behold the glorious image and likeness of the *First I AM* and take it—take it by force! You can experience the *First I AM higher life* today!

CHAPTER 6

LIVING THE *FIRST IAM*

In the last chapter, we discovered how God separates us for himself so we can experience the *First IAM higher self life*. We discovered that the *First IAM higher self life* is one full of blessing, longevity, prosperity, health, favor, grace, and gratitude. We learned that God wants each and every one of his children to experience the abundant life—a life that was demonstrated through the *higher life* of Christ.In this chapter, we will take a brief look at what it means to live within our *First IAM* self image, body, and mind.

Following the *I AM*

Matthew 4:18-22 says,

> Jesus, walking by the sea of Galilee, saw two brethren, Simon called Peter, and Andrew his brother, casting a net into the sea: for they were fishers. And he saith unto them, Follow me, and I will make you fishers of men. And they straightway left their nets, and followed him.
>
> And going on from thence, he saw other two brethren, James the son of Zebedee, and John his brother, in a ship with Zebedee their father, mending their nets; and he called them. And they immediately left the ship and their father, and followed him. (KJV)

Luke 5:27-28 says,

> And after these things he went forth, and saw a publican, named Levi, sitting at the receipt of custom: and he said unto him, Follow me. And he left all, rose up, and followed him. (KJV)

John 1:43 says,

> The day following Jesus would go forth into Galilee, and findeth Philip, and saith unto him, Follow me. (KJV)

Six men; five fishermen and one a tax collector by trade, left their families, their familial inheritances, and their life-long occupations, all to follow after a man they just met. Why? Why would these seemingly intelligent men make such a bold move?

Jesus had something—something of great value! Jesus was the very essence and energy of the Creator! Jesus embodied God! Jesus was filled to the brim with the *I AM*.

Moses didn't have what Jesus had. Abraham didn't have what Jesus had. The Greek gods didn't possess what Jesus had. Today, we would say that Jesus had the *it* factor. Whatever God is in totality—Jesus had *it*. And these six men wanted what Jesus had!

Romans 1:19-20 says,

> For that which is known about God is evident to them and made plain in their [mankind's] inner consciousness, because God [Himself] has shown it to them.
>
> For ever since the creation of the world His invisible nature and attributes, that is, His eternal power and divinity, have been made intelligible and clearly discernible in and through the things that have been made. (AMP)

Colossians 1:15-17 says,

> Christ is the exact likeness of the unseen God [the visible representation of the invisible]; He is the Firstborn [image of God] of all creation. For it was in Him that all things were created, in heaven and on earth, things seen and things unseen, whether thrones, dominions, rulers, or authorities; all things were created and exist through Him [by His service, intervention] and in and for Him. And He Himself existed before all things, and in Him all things consist (cohere, are held together). (AMP)

Christ is the *it*—and the *it* is the invisible exact reflection and resemblance of God. Christ possesses all the attributes of God as demonstrated through his words, his deeds, his actions, his attitude, his love, his grace, his countenance, his demeanor, his *e-v-e-r-y-t-h-i-n-g* displays the *higher mind* of Spirit!

As we discovered earlier, Christ is the *he him* of Genesis 1:27a. Christ is the *first* part of our constitution which represents both *spirit and flesh.*[127] Christ is the *highest* part of our *inner consciousness* which is transfigured by God's Spirit. Christ, if we receive *he him*, becomes our *divine self* in the flesh.

Romans 8:10-17 says,

> Anyone, of course, who has not welcomed this invisible but clearly present God, the Spirit of Christ, won't know what we're talking about.
>
> When God lives and breathes in you (and he does, as surely as he did in Jesus), you are delivered from that dead life. With his Spirit living in you, your body will be as alive as Christ's!
>
> So don't you see that we don't owe this old do-it-yourself life one red cent. There's nothing in it for us, nothing at all. The best thing

[127] John 3:5-6

> to do is give it a decent burial and get on with your new life. God's Spirit beckons. There are things to do and places to go!

This resurrection life you received from God is not a timid, grave-tending life. It's adventurously expectant, greeting God with a childlike "What's next, Papa?" God's Spirit touches our spirits and confirms who we really are. We know who he is, and we know who we are: Father and children. And we know we are going to get what's coming to us—an unbelievable inheritance! (MSG)

Our *highest self* has no material lineage, as was the case with Christ. Our *highest self* is spirit and spirit has no beginning and no ending. While it is true that our physical body finds it's origination in this earth (a material ancestral line), our spirit *self* finds its beginning (genesis) in Spirit![128]

Hebrews 1:1-3; 15-19 says,

> Melchizedek was king of Salem and priest of the Highest God. He met Abraham, who was returning from "the royal massacre," and gave him his blessing.[129] Abraham in turn gave him a tenth of the spoils.
>
> "Melchizedek" means "King of Righteousness." "Salem" means "Peace." So, he is also "King of Peace." Melchizedek *towers out of the past—without record of family ties, no account of beginning or end.* In *this way he is like the Son of God*, one huge priestly presence dominating the landscape always.
>
> The Melchizedek story provides a perfect analogy: Jesus, a priest like Melchizedek, *not by genealogical descent but by the sheer force of resurrection life—he lives!*—"priest forever in the royal order of Melchizedek." The former way of doing things, a system of commandments that never worked out the way it was supposed

---

128 Genesis 1:27; 2:7

129 Genesis 14:18-20

> to, was set aside; the law brought nothing to maturity. Another way—Jesus!—a way that does work, that brings us right into the presence of God, is put in its place. (MSG)

Our *highest self* has no need for a *record of family ties—no account of beginning or end—no genealogical descent.* Our *highest self* is God (Spirit) and God is the *I AM that I AM*. God is universal and eternal, not temporal and limited.[130] God doesn't change.[131] Thus, our *highest self image* doesn't either. Our true *self* has never changed. Though our bodies change constantly—though our lives change with the current of the winds—though our lower minds change with the current of the tides—our *highest self image and likeness is constant!* How refreshing to know that our true *self* is something we can rely on—depend on—call upon in our moment of need![132] Christ relied upon and called upon his *higher self image* for all things.[133]

Christ is our *highest* benchmark—standard bearer—the *highest* example of God's image and likeness on earth. If we will but follow after his example which is our *highest* example, we will enjoy the *higher life* God has planned for us since before the world was created![134] God has destined us to be conformed—renewed into this *higher standard*—this very image and likeness.[135]

Galatians 5:24 tells us that those who receive their *First IAM self image* and *identity* (Christ) have crucified their old fleshly, godless, human natures. Its passions, appetites, and desires are no longer able to deceive us and entice us. It's as if we are dead to the old ways—we are dead to our old ways if we are authentically living in and by our Christ mind!

Paul, when describing his own lower self death and resurrection, had this to say in Philippians 3:10,

---

130 Isaiah 40:28

131 Malachi 3:6

132 Psalm 46:1

133 John 5:19

134 Ephesians 1:4

135 Romans 8:29

> [For my determined purpose is] that I may know *Him* [that I may progressively become more deeply and intimately acquainted with *Him*, perceiving and recognizing and understanding the wonders of *His Person* (identity) more strongly and more clearly], and that I may in that same way come to know the power outflowing from *His* resurrection, and that I may so share *His* sufferings as to be continually transformed [in spirit into *His likeness* even] to His death, [in the hope] (AMP)

When we are living by our *highest identity*, the lower and base parts of our brain no longer control our actions and emotions. The Christ demonstrated, through his death, burial, and resurrection that we have the ability and power to resurrect from the ashes of our old lives. We have the authority to overthrow those old strongholds and unhealthy habitual practices that once held us hostage to oppression, disease, illness, and mental disorder. Through the Christ *higher identity*, we can begin the rebuilding and renewing process of our *mind, body,* and *life!* Our *highest objective*, like that of Paul's, is to become like Christ in every way, including the crucifixion of our old fleshly identities, in order to experience our *higher life* in God!

Hearing the *I AM*

John 10:27-30 says,

> My sheep hear my voice, and I know them, and they follow me: And I give unto them eternal life; and they shall never perish, neither shall any man pluck them out of my hand. My Father, which gave them me, is greater than all; and no man is able to pluck them out of my Father's hand. I and my Father are one. (KJV)

In Matthew's gospel, in the thirteenth chapter, Jesus is telling a crowd of people a parable about finding their true identity and divine design for their lives. What's useful to our study is the fact that he uses a seed and the sowing of that seed into four types of soil as a metaphor to drive home his message.

The parable of Jesus is as follows:

> Behold, a sower went out to sow. And as he sowed, some seed fell by the wayside; and the birds came and devoured them. Some fell on stony places, where they did not have much earth; and they immediately sprang up because they had no depth of earth. But when the sun was up they were scorched, and because they had no root they withered away. And some fell among thorns, and the thorns sprang up and choked them. But others fell on good ground and yielded a crop: some a hundredfold, some sixty, some thirty. He who has ears to hear let him hear! (KJV)

Notice that Jesus ends his lesson with the words, *he who has ears to hear let him hear.* Spiritual ideas can only be heard by spiritual ears, seen with spiritual eyes, and spoken into existence with a spiritual tongue, all of which are attached to a spiritual neck and head. You cannot read your Bible with your fleshly eyes and ears and expect to see and hear what only your spiritual eyes and ears are capable of seeing and hearing. And you certainly cannot expect your mouth to speak God's truth into existence for your life while making negative confessions with the same tongue.

And by the way, your spiritual eyes and ears cannot operate without the right signals generated and processed by your *higher mind.* God is the intelligence behind the intelligence. Just as neurotransmitters send and receive messages between brain cells in your human brain, so, too, are spiritual messengers of God sent to bring enlightenment to you in the form of wisdom and discernment as you begin to employ your *higher mind.*

Now, a spiritual head comes equipped with at least two spiritual ears and two spiritual eyes. You have the *right* to employ your spiritual ears which are attached to your spiritual head. Perhaps no one has ever told you that you have spiritual ears or a spiritual head. Well, congratulations—you have both—all you have to do is simply make the choice to use them.

Getting used to your new ears and new eyes will take some practice, however; a serious commitment on your part is necessary, or as Jesus' parable asserts, your new found wisdom and understanding will fall by the wayside, get burned up, or choked out, forfeiting your spiritual inheritance altogether.

And what is your spiritual inheritance, you ask? Your spiritual inheritance is complete mental, physical, and spiritual wholeness—which is the perfect will of God. When you are mentally and physically whole—you are able to carry out the blueprint of your divine design—which is why you were created in the first place! It is within your divine design that you find the most pleasure and life success![136] However, without spiritual wisdom and discernment you can forget about it. You have to have God's mind if you're going to take hold of your *right mind.*

Now, Jesus' parable goes on to say that as the sower of the seed went about broadcasting the seed, some of the seed fell by the *wayside*, some on *stony places*, some on *thorny ground,* and some on *good ground.*

The *seed* which the sower is sowing is the *word of the kingdom.* The *word* employed by Jesus in this instance is the Greek word *logos.* The word *logos* is defined as *a conception or idea; the mental faculty of thinking, meditating, reasoning, calculating, the divine reason or plan of God.*

A Greek philosopher named Heraclitus first used the term *logos* around 600 B.C. to designate the divine reason or plan which coordinates a changing universe.[137] According to Philo of Alexandria, the *logos* represented the overall divine plan of God. Certain Christian apologists believed the Christ to be the physical manifestation of the *Logos;* demonstrating the divine plan of God through word and deed. They also describe the Spirit of God as an intangible and illuminating influence, such as light emanating from a flame.[138]

---

136 Revelation 4:11

137 "Logos" Strong's Enhanced Lexicon, #3056

138 Athenagoras, Early Christian Apologist

The divine plan of God [logos seed] is being introduced [sown] to the physical minds of men all the time.[139] This makes perfect sense, considering that all thoughts, whether good or bad, are filtered and processed via our physical brains [earthly soil]. However, without the illuminating influence of the Spirit, the rehabilitating and regenerative process and message of God is lost. It has nowhere to take root. Memory must be formed and processed in a very specific way by our brains or else it gets moved to the recesses of our minds and forgotten.[140] We call this kind of memory short-term memory.

What we as spiritual beings need our brains to do is create long-term memory where God's *logos* is concerned. We need to create solid and long lasting memories of God's wisdom and discernment as we are imbued with revelation. The only way to retain God's *logos* [seed] within our memory banks [brain soil] is to meditate upon God's word continually.[141]

According to Jesus' parable concerning the soil along the *wayside,* when we attempt to receive the wisdom and understanding of God via another path—via another way—we are sadly mistaken. The *wayside* is a path or a road situated to the side of the garden. Number one, a pathway or a road isn't the proper soil for growing produce or whatever seed is being planted. A pathway or road is worn down and packed hard by foot traffic. Why on earth would Spirit waste good seed on a worn pathway or side road rather than good rich soil? Second, there is only one way or one path to God and that is through the mind of Spirit.[142] Spiritual growth and development cannot be attained through another person. Don't be deceived by thinking that listening to brother super Christian down at the local church is going to make you *wise unto wholeness.*[143]

139 Romans 1:20

140 Dr. Caroline Leaf, *Who Switched Off My Brain? Controlling Toxic Thoughts and Emotions,* Switch on Your Brain USA, Inc. July 2008

141 Psalm 119

142 John 14:6; 1 Corinthians 2

143 2 Timothy 3:15

Look, prior to God's promise made to Abraham in chapter twelve, Genesis 11:31-32 tells us:

And Terah took Abram his son, and Lot the son of Haran his son's son, and Sarai his daughter in law, his son Abram's wife; and they went forth with them from Ur of the Chaldees, to go into the land of Canaan; and they came unto Haran, and dwelt there. And the days of Terah were two hundred and five years: and Terah died in Haran. (KJV)

What you may or may not know is this; Terah and his family never made it to Canaan. It was Abraham who took his family the rest of the way into Canaan. You see, our familial systems and our clergy can only take us so far in our very personal spiritual evolutionary journey. We, being led by the divine mind, must go the rest of the journey alone. No one can take your spiritual journey for you! Not even Jesus![144] You and God must go it alone![145]

You will never receive spiritual wisdom or understanding via a third party. All you will ever receive via a third party [wayside] is *some* spiritual head knowledge. Understand this: head knowledge isn't the same as spiritual wisdom and understanding—not even close. Third party bible head knowledge, wayside knowledge, is simply short-term spiritual memory. It won't take root. It can't take root. It doesn't have the right soil to do so. The *higher mind*, a mind fixed on God, a mind that meditates upon the word of God continually, is the right soil!

Believing the *I AM*

Seeds are planted down in the earth. God's image is planted down in you. Finding your God *higher identity* and *higher self image* is a matter of positioning. Stop looking outward and start looking inward. It's so easy to believe that God is up there or out there somewhere rather than between your ears and behind your eyes.

---

144 John 3:7, 5:6

145 Genesis 22:5; Matthew 4:1; 14:23; 26:40; Mark 6:46; Luke 9:18

From the time you were born until you were old enough to know better (or at least contemplate), you were told that what you see is all that exists. Interestingly enough, your thoughts can't be seen, and yet you still believe they exist. Your memories are invisible, and yet you still remember. Now, stop and think about what we just said. Your thoughts are invisible. Your thoughts are down in you. You carry them with you all day long. They're even operating while you sleep.

God's presence in your life works the very same way. Spirit is invisible. Spirit is down in you. You carry Spirit with you all day long. Spirit is operating while you sleep. So where's the disconnect? Why do you keep seeking God from a purely external position? Turn inward. Look inside. God is inside you. God is operating within your body *already*! You are Spirit!

Hebrews 11:1 says,

> Faith is the confidence that what we hope for will actually happen; it gives us assurance about things we cannot see. (NLT)

The truth is; we all have a type of faith—albeit, it may not be a God-type-faith. When we allow our lower minds to roam without deliberate intention or thought-life awareness, we believe, or employ a type of faith, in all the *what-if* scenarios our fear-mongering and irrational minds can conjure up. Not only do we believe these false negative confessions, we actually help them come into existence through the ignorance of our mouths. Our mouth has power and it was given to us by God as a means to co-create with God. Our mouth was never intended to be used to curse our own minds, bodies, and lives. Our mouth was created to speak God-things into existence and lead us into complete wholeness![146]

It takes the employment of the *higher mind* of God to move further away from one's old habits and thought patterns, which keep us in the

[146] Romans 10:10

perpetual and deadly practice of defining our self and others by our former ignorant and harmful delineations and unattainable, unnatural, unfruitful, and unnecessary standards and burdens. The *higher self image* renders these worldly and unreal designations useless and senseless, and makes us aware of their uselessness and senselessness so that we stop repeating them and living by their false laws.

How many times have we heard people complain about the holidays and the absolute whippin' it is when they try to please their familial systems? Why do we allow ourselves to suffer so around the holiday season? It appears that we suffer because we're trying to please others who frankly, are never pleased.

When God said to Abraham (Abram at the time),

> Leave your country, your family, and your relatives and go to the land that I will show you. I will bless you and make your descendants into a great nation. You will become famous and be a blessing to others. (MSG)

Abraham didn't respond to God's promise with, "You know what God, I think I'll pass."

The text says,

> So Abram departed, as the LORD had spoken unto him. (MSG)

Abraham didn't sit around and wait for someone to tell him how he *felt* about God's promise—he simply acted. He got his wife and their things and headed out immediately. Do you know why Abraham *departed* immediately? Abraham *heard* God.

The text doesn't say that Abram *felt* God; it says Abram departed, as the LORD had *spoken unto him.* God gave you two ears and two eyes for a reason. Just as your ears and eyes take in information for your brain to process and thereby operate your physical body, so, too, God uses your spiritual ears and eyes to operate the spiritual body.[147] Just as your physical body is made up trillions of cells, so too, is the body of Spirit which is made up of an undeterminable amount of spiritual offspring. You are one of the multitudes of cells in the body of Spirit.

Stop looking around you for the *right people* or the *right circumstances* to make you *feel* good about who you are and your choices in life. Start looking within yourself for your true self worth—your true *higher self* image, your true *higher First IAM identity*—and find the *higher mind* of God and *hear* what the Spirit is saying about you and to you. Walk in that affirmation as opposed to your emotions or, worse still, the emotions of others and their false words, ideas, and designations that do not define you!

Don't misunderstand our message: we're not advocating familial estrangement. There are some people who derive a great deal of pleasure from their family systems. Great for you if you are one of those individuals! Some family systems are very healthy and allow one another space to grow and thus develop healthily. Some family systems even encourage personal growth and that's wonderful. Regardless of the family system, one must find one's God ears and eyes, aside from one's natural ears and eyes, which may or may not be attached to a familial head (mindset).

Make sure that your eyes and ears are attached to the *right head* and you'll never be faced with another tormenting Thanksgiving and Christmas holiday season ever again! When you're no longer bound by those old familial identities or designations—designations which once held you hostage to your emotions and old psychological toxic thinking patterns and energies—you are free to be the true you: the *First IAM* you!

Shouting at Jericho and Slaying the Giant!

In the first few chapters of the book of Joshua, we see the children of Israel preparing to take the heavily fortified and wealthy city of

147 1 Corinthians 12

Jericho. In their quest to take possession of Canaan, the Israelites were instructed by God not to fight for themselves or seek riches for self aggrandizement, but to be used of God—as his instruments to execute the perfect will of God.

Joshua 6:1-5 says,

> Now Jericho was straitly shut up because of the children of Israel: none went out, and none came in. And the LORD said unto Joshua, See, I have given into thine hand Jericho, and the king thereof, and the mighty men of valour. And ye shall compass the city, all ye men of war, and go round about the city once. Thus shalt thou do six days. And seven priests shall bear before the ark seven trumpets of rams' horns: and the seventh day ye shall compass the city seven times, and the priests shall blow with the trumpets. And it shall come to pass, that when they make a long blast with the ram's horn, and when ye hear the sound of the trumpet, all the people shall shout with a great shout; and the wall of the city shall fall down flat, and the people shall ascend up every man straight before him. (KJV)

The Israelites did as Joshua had commanded. They marched around that great city seven days in a row and on the seventh, the walls fell when they shouted!

What circumstances or strongholds are keeping you locked away from your *highest life* and good? Perhaps, like the Israelites, you should try shouting at your Jericho! Did it ever occur to you that your own negative confessions and thought-life could be preventing you from God's best—your *highest self* and *life?*

Recall, if you will, how Jesus overcame his temptation.[148] He spoke God's truth to the tempter—to the adversarial spirit of Belial![149]

[148] Matthew 4:1-11

[149] Belial is the personification of worthlessness

Jesus deflected every false accusation hurled at him and you can too! You must if you are to experience the *First IAM higher mind, body,* and *life.*

First Samuel 17:42-48 says,

> And when the Philistine looked around and saw David, he scorned and despised him, for he was but an adolescent, with a healthy reddish color and a fair face.
>
> And the Philistine said to David, Am I a dog, that you should come to me with sticks? And the Philistine cursed David by his gods. The Philistine said to David, Come to me, and I will give your flesh to the birds of the air and the beasts of the field.
>
> *Then said David* to the Philistine, You come to me with a sword, a spear, and a javelin, but I come to you in the name of the Lord of hosts, the God of the ranks of Israel, Whom you have defied. This day the Lord will deliver you into my hand, and I will smite you and cut off your head. And I will give the corpses of the army of the Philistines this day to the birds of the air and the wild beasts of the earth, that all the earth may know that there is a God in Israel. And all this assembly shall know that the Lord saves not with sword and spear; for the battle is the Lord's, and He will give you into our hands.
>
> When the Philistine came forward to meet David, *David ran quickly toward the battle line to meet the Philistine.* (AMP)

We love this story. It speaks volumes to our own lives. How many times are we faced with a seemingly impossible circumstance? We face challenges many times; daily in fact. Even if we had no physical enemies, the Goliath's of our own minds calling out to us—taunting us—would be enough. Check out what David did when faced with Goliath's challenge.

David said,

> You come to me with a sword, a spear, and a javelin, but I come to you in the name of the Lord of hosts, the God of the ranks of Israel, Whom you have defied. (NLT)

First Samuel 17:12 says,

> Now David was the son of a man named Jesse, an Ephrathite from Bethlehem in the land of Judah. (NLT)

David didn't come at Goliath in his father's name—his earthly identity. No, David invoked his *First I AM* identity; an identity he took for himself! David understood just how powerful his *higher identity* was and boldly tested its power in front of all of Israel's military and his commander in chief. David was more than confident—David was the *First I AM* in action!

Watch what David does when the giant comes charging his way. David runs toward his opponent. David didn't wait and aim his sling shot at Goliath—David ran toward the battle line. Not only did David run; he ran *quickly*. We are almost positive that David ran at his Jericho with his mouth professing God's effectual word all the way!

Romans 4:17 says,

> God, who quickeneth the dead, and calleth those things which be not as though they were. (KJV)

David told his giant just how the battle was going to end. David knew that the battle was God's. David also knew that God doesn't lose battles. David proclaimed God's plan from the beginning. David believed that the voice of the *First I AM* within was greater than the lower voices of some uncircumcised Philistine.

Shout at your Jericho affirmatively, assertively, confidently, and courageously! You are called by the *highest name* of all names! You were created in the very image and likeness of the *highest God!* Shout at the walls of division; walls that are keeping you from your greatest riches. Lest you forget, within the walls of Jericho were great treasures, treasures that were meant to be used in the service of the LORD.[150] Inside of you resides tremendous value, value to be used in the service of the *I AM.*

Do you remember what God told the Israelites back in Deuteronomy 6:10-11?

The text reads,

> And it shall be, when the LORD thy God shall have brought thee into the land which he sware unto thy fathers, to Abraham, to Isaac, and to Jacob, to give thee great and goodly cities, which thou buildedst not, And houses full of all good things, which thou filledst not, and wells digged, which thou diggedst not, vineyards and olive trees, which thou plantedst not; when thou shalt have eaten and be full. (KJV)

When we shout at our Jericho's, we make Deuteronomy 6:10-11 a reality for our own lives! Your *higher* authority, your *higher self* full of great things, your *higher mind* which springs forth without ceasing or going dry, your *higher body* which keeps producing in season and out of season, are all waiting for you to assert your *First IAM identity! Speak to your Jericho*!!!

Florence Scovel Shinn created a wonderful affirmation; an affirmation that all people should proclaim daily—as often as one remembers to do so. It goes like this,

---

[150] Joshua 6:19

> The walls of lack and delay now crumble away and I enter my Promised Land under grace.[151]

It is our sincere prayer and objective that the walls of your Jericho come tumbling down! May you know your *highest self*—the *First I AM—today*!

[151] Florence Scovel Shinn, *The Game of Life & The Secret Door to Success,* (Axiom Publishing, 2004), 68

Chapter 7

FREEDOM IN THE *FIRST IAM*

The Frankl Factor

Viktor Frankl, MD, PhD was an Austrian neurolo gist and psychiatrist who survived the Nazi Holocaust.[152] In his celebrated book, *Man's Search for Meaning*, Dr. Frankl records his harrowing experiences in the Nazi death camps and how he was determined to find man's reason for living.

We were personally struck by Dr. Frankl's poignant and eloquent words as he describes his struggle to find meaning and purpose while in the depths of his own struggle for survival. He writes,

> We stumbled on in the darkness, over big stones and through large puddles, along the one road leading from the camp. The accompanying guards kept shouting at us and driving us with the butts of their rifles. Anyone with very sore feet supported himself on his neighbor's arm. Hardly a word was spoken; the icy wind did not encourage talk. Hiding his mouth behind his upturned collar, the man marching next to me whispered suddenly: "If our wives could see us now! I do hope they are better off in their camps and don't know what is happening to us."

152 "Viktor Frankl," *Wikipedia, the Free Encyclopedia,* http://en.wikipedia.org/w/index.php?title=Viktor_Frankl&oldid=438914158 (accessed May 2011)

That brought thoughts of my own wife to mind. And as we stumbled on for miles, slipping on icy spots, supporting each other time and again, dragging one another up and onward, nothing was said, but we both knew: each of us was thinking of his wife. Occasionally I looked at the sky, where the stars were fading and the pink light of the morning was beginning to spread behind a dark bank of clouds. But my mind clung to my wife's image, imagining it with an uncanny acuteness. I heard her answering me, saw her smile, her frank and encouraging look. Real or not, her look was then more luminous than the sun which was beginning to rise.

A thought transfixed me: for the first time in my life I saw the truth as it is set into song by so many poets, proclaimed as the final wisdom by so many thinkers. The truth—that love is the ultimate and the highest goal to which man can aspire. Then I grasped the meaning of the greatest secret that human poetry and human thought and belief have to impart: The salvation of man is through love and in love. I understood how a man who has nothing left in this world still may know bliss, be it only for a brief moment, in the contemplation of his beloved. In a position of utter desolation, when man cannot express himself in positive action, when his only achievement may consist in enduring his sufferings in the right way—an honorable way—in such a position man can, through loving contemplation of the image he carries of his beloved, achieve fulfillment. For the first time in my life I was able to understand the meaning of the words, "The angels are lost in perpetual contemplation of an infinite glory . . . "[153]

Just as Dr. Frankl imagined the glorious image of his beloved in order to endure and survive the cruel and ruthless conditions of his horrific ordeal, we too must hold fast to our *First I AM* self image if we are to endure and survive the cruel and harsh conditions and circumstances

[153] Viktor Frankl, *Man's Search for Meaning* (New York: Beacon Press, 2006), 37-38

of our own death camps. Our *First IAM* self is our *beloved.* The most *sacred self* of our constitution is the very image and likeness of God—the *lover of our soul.*

The Song of Solomon 2:16-17 puts it like this,

> My lover is mine, and I am his. Nightly he strolls in our garden; delighting in the flowers until dawn breathes its light and night slips away. Turn to me, dear lover. (MSG)

God's image and likeness, like an eager lover, is waiting for us to acknowledge its presence within our being. Viktor Frankl said that *love is the ultimate and the highest goal to which man can aspire . . . the salvation of man is through love and in love. Love* resides within each and every human being; waiting to be believed, accepted, and received with gladness and gratitude.

Man's highest purpose and meaning for life is to find this *love* in order to be the reflection of God's glorious image and likeness in the earth as it is in heaven. Our ultimate purpose in life is to live and breathe and have our being-ness in God's glorious image and likeness. As we do this, we begin the process of bringing God's kingdom into reality, not only for our individual lives, but for the corporate life of all others on planet earth.

Matthew 22:37-40 says,

> Love the Lord your God with all your passion and prayer and intelligence. This is the most important, the first on any list. But there is a second to set alongside it: Love others as well as you love yourself. These two commands are pegs; everything in God's Law and the Prophets hangs from them. (MSG)

Love is the essential rule of God's economy—not a list of do's—not a list of don'ts—love! Love is the over-arching rule of God's meaning and design for our individual lives! Just as Dr. Frankl asserted, *love is the ultimate and the highest goal to which man can aspire.* It is love which transforms, renews, regenerates, and revitalizes all life!

The *First IAM higher life* mission is to help others find their *highest life* and *highest self image*—which is to find *love*. However, we can't very well fulfill this mandate without *First* finding our own *I AM mind, body,* and *self.* The *I AM* is this *love.*[154]

True Liberation Will Come!

Bondage is bondage and hopelessness is hopelessness—it's all relative, really. Viktor Frankl had this to say about man's suffering relativity,

> To draw an analogy: a man's suffering is similar to the behavior of gas. If a certain quantity of gas is pumped into an empty chamber, it will fill the chamber completely and evenly, no matter how big the chamber. Thus, suffering completely fills the human soul and conscious mind, no matter whether the suffering is great or little. Therefore the "size" of human suffering is absolutely relative.[155]

Sadly, in many cases, we have been so victimized and tormented by our societal and religious wardens that we have forgotten what liberation, pleasure, joy, and peace feel like. In every man resides both good and evil—until he finds real meaning and purpose for his life. When individuals find their truest and highest callings, all suffering ceases and the fear of loss quite literally loosens its desperate grip on the material life.[156] The old adage, *life isn't fair,* no longer rings true—for life becomes the fairest and the brightest when all find their *highest self* and *highest life* in God!

God has a wonderful and brilliant plan for your life.[157] Be patient. Change takes time. Give yourself room for expansion—allow for

---

154 1 John 4:8

155 Viktor Frankl, *Man's Search for Meaning* (New York: Beacon Press, 2006), 44

156 1 John 4:18

157 Habakkuk 2:3

mistakes; the eventual ebb and flow of life. Cut yourself some slack and try not to become so serious while growing and developing in your new *higher self image*. God has a delightful sense of humor even though we don't always appreciate it. God wants you to laugh again—smile again—love again. God has a new *mind, body*, and *life* waiting just for you! Receive it today!

Living within the reality of your *higher First IAM life* will take commitment and dedication on your part.

Hebrews 12:11 says,

> No discipline is enjoyable while it is happening—it's painful! But afterward there will be a peaceful harvest of right living for those who are trained in this way. (NLT)

No one likes to train for a marathon or a triathlon. But training is needful if one intends to finish well.

First Corinthians 9:25 says,

> All athletes are disciplined in their training. They do it to win a prize that will fade away, but we do it for an eternal prize. (NLT)

Second Corinthians 10:4-5 says,

> For the arms of our warfare [are] not fleshly, but powerful according to God to [the] overthrow of strongholds; overthrowing reasoning's and every high thing that lifts itself up against the knowledge of God, and leading captive every thought into the obedience of the Christ. (DARBY)

God's word is our strongest weapon against the taunts and false accusations of our lower minds. Just reading the Bible isn't enough! *God's word in our mouths is the most powerful energy force in the universe!* God's word in your mouth will transform your mind! God's word in your mouth will transform your body! God's word in your mouth will transform your self image! Simply put, God's word in your mouth will transform your life! David understood this truth! Joshua understood this truth! Abraham understood this truth! Paul understood this truth! Jesus lived this truth and so can you! You can change your life in a nanosecond by speaking God's word to your current Jericho and giant.

To help get you started, here are a few daily affirmations that you can use:

> *I AM* the seed of God and the higher things of life are my natural birthright! (Genesis 1:28-29)
>
> *I AM* the living and breathing expression of God's powerful Spirit! (Genesis 2:7)
>
> I AM awake and open to God's divine design for my perfect life! (1 Corinthians 2:16)
>
> *I AM* free from all limiting thoughts, strongholds, designs, and attitudes! (2 Corinthians 10:4)
>
> *I AM* full of God's compassion, empathy, and joy, and peace! (Romans 13:8)
>
> *I AM* open to and gladly receive God's promised abundance and provision for my life! (Genesis 12:2)
>
> *I AM* right where *I AM* supposed to be and open to God's divine and perfect will for my life direction! (Romans 12:2)
>
> *I AM* more than capable because God's wisdom is always with me! (Deuteronomy 31:6)
>
> *I AM* fully aware of *who* and *what I AM*, and *I AM* alive! (1 Corinthians 8:6)

Feel free to create your own affirmations. As a matter of fact, we strongly suggest you do. No one knows your life like you do. Align God's word with your own life and see what happens next! We suggest reciting your affirmations at the very least twice a day. We urge you to place God's powerful messages about your *higher identity* wherever and all over.

Deuteronomy 6:4-9 says,

> Listen, Israel! The LORD our God is the only true God! So love the LORD your God with all your heart, soul, and strength. Memorize his laws and tell them to your children over and over again. Talk about them all the time, whether you're at home or walking along the road or going to bed at night, or getting up in the morning. Write down copies and tie them to your wrists and foreheads to help you obey them. Write these laws on the door frames of your homes and on your town gates. (CEV)

Using God's word for your daily meditation and affirmation practice will transform your life—literally!

Shout at your Jericho! Speak to your Goliath! Do whatever you have to do to experience your *First IAM higher self image, mind, body,* and *life!*

Blessings to the *First IAM* in us *all*!

About the Authors

Melissa Dunn is a certified personal growth and spiritual life coach, a certified personal trainer, a certified weight loss management consultant, and a certified sports nutrition consultant. She has spent the majority of her working career in both the medical and pharmaceutical industries. With well over 80,000 hours of biblical and religious study and twenty plus years of medical knowledge under her belt, Melissa has discovered that her true passion is teaching and writing about the importance of the mind-body-spirit connection. Currently, Melissa resides and is in private practice in the Dallas/Fort Worth metroplex.

Leah Dunn earned her bachelor's degree in psychology from Texas Christian University in 1991. Although she thought her path would lead her to becoming a clinical therapist, she began a successful career in the world of finance. Leah is presently a real estate broker and writer and resides in the Dallas/Fort Worth metroplex.

NOTES